# Become A Honey-Do Man

## Turn Your
## Handy-Around-The-Home Skills
## Into CASH!!!

By Kenneth R. Whitaker
The Honey-Do Man
www.The-Honey-Do-Man.com

# Disclaimer

I am not a lawyer, nor do I play one on TV. Even if I were, I probably wouldn't be a lawyer in your state. Do not use any of the forms or documents in this package without getting them approved by a lawyer.

Nor am I an accountant, a tax expert, or a licensed home inspector, plumber or electrician. You should ask your own professionals for help.

We do not guarantee that you will get any gigs, or promise how much money you might make. Your results depend on your own abilities, effort, knowledge, and persistence.

This package, including its documents and any software, is provided as is, without warranty of any kind, whether express or implied, including the implied warranties of merchantability or fitness for a particular purpose. In no event will the author, publisher, or distributors (collectively, the providers) be liable to you for any special, consequential, indirect, or similar damages. In no case shall the providers' liability exceed one dollar. By your use of this package you acknowledge that you agree to these terms and agree not to hold the providers liable for any errors, omissions, mistakes or negligence in the documents in this package.

# Table Of Contents

## *PART ONE*

on page 5

**Getting Started**

Why would ANYBODY pay for an easy job like furniture assembly?

How to charge. How much to charge. How to accept credit cards.

Documents. Get the lady to sign on the dotted line.

Do some basic advertising to get a few gigs. And get a few bucks.

## *PART TWO*

on page 35

**A Hundred Jobs You Can Do, And How to UPSELL!**

You've done many different jobs, but you never made a list before.

Should you go install two mini blinds? Is it worth your trouble? It is if you can find other jobs that you can do. Fix that loose handrail, install new grab bars, and replace a bedroom ceiling light fixture with a paddle fan.

## *PART THREE*

on page 74

**Jack Of All Trades, And Master Of ONE**

You need a specialty, too. You can assemble furniture as well as the next guy. But what if you got REALLY good at it? Learn a few tricks, buy a few tools that the average guy won't buy. Target your advertising.

# *PART FOUR*

on page 87

**Tips, Tricks, And Cool Tools**

The Third Hand lets you hang a cabinet with NO hands!

How to cheat at plumbing.

How to install a 4x4 post for a mailbox WITHOUT mixing concrete.

# *PART FIVE*

on page 99

**Marketing**

While you are sitting on your couch, wondering why nobody is calling, read this.

# PART ONE

# Are You Handy?
# Start a Handyman Business,
# Part Time At First.

## *Turning Pro*

You've always been handy around the house. You have assembled furniture, a swing set, and a shed. You have installed ceiling fans, a garage door opener, drape rods, and mini blinds. You have done a little plumbing, a little electrical, and a little drywall. You clean your own gutters, cut your own grass, and blow your own snow. And of course, you have painted.

More importantly, if a job comes up that you have never done before, you are not afraid to give it a shot. Maybe you do a little Internet research, and maybe you buy a new tool. But you DON'T call a pro. Well, maybe you do call, if you KNOW the job is too big, but that's your last resort.

And now you've been thinking about becoming a handyman, even if only part time. You have a lot of tools. You like doing these jobs. Your friends and relatives ask you to do these jobs for them, for free.

Why not turn this hobby into a moneymaker?

## *You Can Start Part Time*

You can work two or three hours, in one evening, doing something that's easy, like assembling furniture.

I charge $39 an hour, for a minimum of two hours, plus a $25 trip charge. That's $103. Let's call it $100, for easy head math.

Can you repeat that one evening every week?

If so, then that comes out to more than $5,000 a year.

Do you have a day job? That's better than the raise you are hoping for at work. Are you looking for a better day job? KEEP your old day job, and do this part time.

And if something happens to your day job...

What if you get laid off, or downsized? You have been doing odd jobs one evening a week. You have your ducks in a row. You can easily crank this up to full time.

## Do More, Make More

It's easy to work more than two hours a week. Can you work FIVE gigs a week? They might be one morning gig, two afternoon gigs, and two on Saturday. Or, if you're keeping your day job, that could be three evenings and two weekend jobs. Either way, five gigs times $100 each is $500 a week. $2000 a month.

Now you're up to $26,000 a year. And you're only working 10 hours!

And many jobs take MORE than two hours. Assembling a desk, chair, and book shelf might take six or even eight hours.

Are you out of work? You can do this while you look for a new job. And when you find that job, you can KEEP doing this, so you can climb back out of the hole.

Or maybe THIS is your new job. Don't FIND a new job! MAKE one!


## Who Will Call You?

I have done all those jobs listed above, and many more, for other people. For money.

You think they are easy jobs. Other people have no idea where to start.

I have been called to assemble something, only to find that the box has already been opened, and a few pieces were already put together. Can you imagine starting such a job, giving up, and calling for help? But what else can these people do? They can't get the parts back into the box, they can't return the item to the store, they can't live with parts spread out all over, and they can't throw the item out. You are their last resort.

Can you imagine such a job taking all day? I assembled a shelving unit with six shelves for an older woman. It took less than an hour. She couldn't believe it. You see, she just assembled a smaller 2-shelf end table, and it took her all day! How could it take all day? She probably got frustrated, quit, watched some TV, and got back to it. Maybe some bourbon was involved.

She would have tried the larger unit, but she couldn't even lift the box.

Most of my customers are NOT competent. And they don't WANT to be, either! All of their tools fit in one shoebox. That shoebox isn't even full.

# There Are Other Reasons

Some people ARE competent and could do their own jobs. But they still call you.

**They could be busy.**

Consider an executive who works ten hours a day and several more hours at home on the weekend. That eats up a lot of time. Would such a person want to waste what little weekend is left assembling a desk? They would rather pay you to do it.

Do this math: If you charge $35 an hour, and take three hours to do something, you made about $100. If you had a full time job at $35 an hour, you'd be making about $70,000 a year. Would this executive think a handyman was worth that?

But your yuppy customer is doing DIFFERENT math: He's making $60 an hour when he's at work. But he KNOWS it would take him TEN hours to assemble that desk! Ten times $60 is more than he spent on the desk! You say you can do it for $100. Ten hours for $100 sounds about right. He doesn't know it will take you LESS than ten hours. You are a BARGAIN!

He'd rather spend some of his excess money and save some of his precious time.

**They could have a deadline.**

Some people are pressed for time. I had one out-of-town couple that was helping their son move into a new apartment for college. They needed a lot of furniture assembled, and they only had one weekend. I assembled a bed frame, a chest of drawers, a nightstand, a couch, an easy chair, an ottoman, a desk, a desk chair, a dining room table, 4 chairs, a coffee table, a TV stand, and a microwave cart. It took a day and a half, but the job was done, their son was ready to start school, and they were on their plane Sunday night.

Other people need something done because they are expecting some company from out-of-town. And they have other things to do before the company arrives.

**Some people are physically challenged.**

I have a customer who has some metal in her neck. She is in pain all the time. Every fall I remove two window air conditioners for her, and every spring I reinstall them. It's not hard for me, but it's impossible for her. I've seen her have difficulty plugging in a lamp.

# There Are Easy Jobs Out There

Power washing is easy. You just stand there and hold a hose. But you need a power washer. Many people would like to clean their own deck, but won't buy a big machine for one job. So why don't YOU go get one?

And now you have another job on your list that you can do.

## *Jobs Get Easier*

Let's say you and your brother each assemble identical computer desks. Let's say it takes each of you three hours. You are no better and no worse than your brother. Both of you are competent, but not especially proficient.

Now let's say you assemble another one, and another, and another. Each time, it gets easier. You learn a few tricks. You buy a few tools. Eventually you will be able to do it in only one hour.

Your brother assembles something every year or two. He has no reason to practice and get better.

And that older woman will NEVER be able to tackle something more complicated than her end table. I have often been asked to complete assemblies for people who started and gave up. It's always exciting to see which pieces they lost.

Now install a ceiling fan. And another. You see? Each job you tackle gets easier, and extends your list of jobs you can do.

## *But Some Jobs Get Harder, Too*

Drywall repair isn't hard, at your own house. You cut the repair piece, screw it in, and apply your tape and mud. While the first coat dries, you go do something else, or even quit until the next day. In fact, there's no rush. You don't even have to come back the next day. You can get around to it when you have time, or when you feel like it. When you do get back to it, you sand the first coat and apply the second coat. Sometimes there's a third coat, too.

Now imagine doing that same job somewhere else. Maybe there is no other job that you could move on to. Maybe you have to make another trip. Maybe even a third trip. And maybe that lady won't appreciate you "getting around to it" while her job is half finished.

Yes, I know about five-minute mud. You can do your first coat, drink a cup of coffee, and do your second coat. I personally don't like it. It's messy and there's too much pressure.

The same thing applies when you need a tool you don't have with you, or if you have to go to the store to buy a part. At home, it's no big deal. You always have ALL your tools with you. You don't even have to go the store right away. No one complains when a job takes 2 days or a week to finish.

That's what this book is about: How to switch from a handy man around the house to a handyman at somebody else's house.

# You Don't Have To Do Every Job

Do you like to paint? But you fail at plumbing? Then don't do the plumbing job!

If you place an ad in your Pennysaver (or Thrifty Nickel, or Bargain Shopper, etc.) that you paint, you won't get a lot of calls for plumbing.

What if someone hires you to paint a room, and asks if you'd do a plumbing job while you're there?

- You could say, "Sorry, I don't do plumbing."

- Or you could say, "I don't do plumbing, but I have a friend who does." And then subcontract it out. You can make money on a job that you don't even do.

- You could consider doing the job, depending on how easy it is. Let's say you never installed a new bathroom vanity. Why not give it a shot? You'd be no better or worse than the average guy out there. And the next one will be easier. And your customer would NEVER give it a shot.

# This Works!

You have tried affiliate marketing. It doesn't work. At least, not for you. You have tried selling soap or vitamins in an MLM. That didn't work either. You have tried several other work-at-home plans, too. The only thing they have in common is that none of them worked for you.

But with this, you will be standing in someone's living room, assembling a new computer desk, turning a screw driver with your own hands. And you will finish. They will have a new computer desk, and you will have $100 in your pocket.

# Avoid Analysis Paralysis

Every book I've ever read about starting a new business always starts with entities. Should you be an S-Corp? An LLC? You can't open a business checking account without an entity. And what about insurance?

I am not a lawyer, nor do I play one on TV. But here's my FREE advice:

> *Go ahead.*
> *Take a chance.*
> *Assemble a bookcase.*
> *What can go wrong?*

What CAN go wrong? Maybe it turns out that you ARE incompetent! You put a shelf in backwards so the unfinished edge is showing. So undo a few steps, turn that shelf around, and proceed. So it took you longer than you expected. But you're done. And you'll get better.

You eventually will need a corporation. What if someone sues you and they come after your personal property?

But for a bookshelf? Really?

What's the WORST that can happen? You damage a part, and now you CAN'T finish the job! You DESTROYED the bookcase! So you reimburse the lady, haul away the parts, and collect NOTHING. But she didn't sue you and try to get your house, did she?

You will need a good legal structure. But you can start today without one. What if you start your corporation, get one gig, and then decide you don't like handy-manning?

And how do you get paid? If the customer makes their check out to your business name (which you haven't even thought up yet), you'll have to open a business account, which you can't do until you establish your entity. So ask them to make their check out to YOU! Or ask for cash!

Yes, you should get official. Eventually. But you can do jobs while you're getting official.

For example, in Pennsylvania, I have to collect and pay sales tax for some jobs. But while I'm starting, I can collect it while I'm applying for my license, and eventually send it in. This is no excuse to procrastinate.

The same goes for licensing. In Pennsylvania, if you make more than $5000 a year or $500 from one customer, you have to register with the attorney general. So you can do quite a few jobs before you have to register. Even if you DON'T register, the worst that happens is that the attorney general gets wind of your activity, calls you, and makes you register.

And so it goes. Do your homework, but get started! Assemble a bookcase! The lady's house will NOT explode or catch fire!

## *Do Your Homework*

Before you go out on your first job, you must think about entities, licensing, insurance, taxes, documents, etc.

Perhaps you can go on some small jobs without DOING any of this. Perhaps you only need to get into this stuff after you get serious.

But at a minimum, you must at least THINK about it.

For example, maybe you can make do without insurance.

A lady wanted me to replace a toilet. I've done it before. I'm not as good as a real plumber, but I can do it.

But this particular toilet was on the second floor. On the floor below was a grand piano!

What if that wax ring falls off as I lower the toilet into place? The ring won't seat, and I won't know. The toilet will leak. The piano will be destroyed.

So I said, "Sorry, lady. You need a real plumber."

It would have been nice to make a buck. But the risk was too high.

You can work without insurance, if you are careful to choose safe jobs. But even with insurance, this job was too risky.

## Local Laws

You need to check your local laws. Do you need a handyman license? Do you NEED insurance? Do you have to pay a business privilege tax?

I can tell you what I did. Don't take this as a list of things that YOU should do.

## Entities

You can start with your own name. You are "John Smith, The Handyman." You are a "sole proprietor". You can open a checking account in your own name, or use your current checking account. People can write checks to "John Smith", but you will be able to deposit a check with the entire name.

You file a Schedule C with your personal taxes. You declare how much money you took in, and how much you spent on supplies, materials, advertising, etc.

Subtract your expenses from your income, and the difference is your profit, which carries over to your 1040.

But you have no liability protection. What if you are sweating a pipe joint, and you start a fire and burn their house down? They can sue you and take YOUR house. P.S. – I don't sweat pipes! I either walk from the job or I cheat. (See part 4)

One step up the food chain is the "Fictitious Name". This is a document you file with your state. It is NOT an entity. They can still take your house. But it gives you a business name, like "The Honey-Do Man". You can take your document to the bank and open an account in that name. People can write you checks made out to that name.

If you want liability protection, you should start an S-Corp or an LLC. But those structures are beyond the scope of this book. And your insurance is your first line of defense.

Just get started first.

## Licensing

This topic DEFINITELY requires local research. But here's what I did:

I need no license to be a handyman. Licenses are required for plumbers and electricians, and technically, I'm not supposed to do ANY jobs in those fields.

I'm not even allowed to change a washer in a faucet! A registered plumber is allowed to, but he must file a report with the department of health! Bureaucrats! Don't you just love them?

I'm a firm believer in the saying:

*"It's better to ask forgiveness than permission."*

And so far, I haven't even needed to ask forgiveness.

I will not remodel a bathroom. But I will replace a vanity and sink. I do jobs that the average homeowner can do. Many stores sell this stuff to the public.

But I DID have to register with Pennsylvania's Attorney General. If you are a "Home Improvement Contractor" in PA who makes $5,000 a year or has a customer who paid more than $500, you have to register. I flunk both tests. I make more than $5,000 a year and I have customers who paid me more than $500.

And they make you get insurance, too, before they'll register you.

I have to put my registration number on all my contracts and advertising. The Pennysaver won't even take my ad without that number.

# *Insurance*

Insurance was harder to get.

Insurance companies offer "Artisan" insurance. They have roofer insurance, plumber insurance, and electrician insurance. A roofer might fall off a roof, but a plumber is unlikely to. A plumber might do a bad job and cause an indoor flood, destroying hardwood floors, but an electrician is unlikely to. An electrician, well, you get the idea.

But a handyman might be up on a roof AND might replace an outlet AND might replace a sink. We need insurance for ALL these risks. My own insurance man wouldn't issue it at all, for any price.

But I did find it. I got "Contractor" insurance. I pay $450 a year. I have $1 million per incident and $3 million cumulative. I could burn your house down and be covered.

My first year, I bought insurance because I thought I had to. Don't you see "Fully Insured" in the ads? Wouldn't people expect it? Well, not one person asked to see it! So I let it lapse, and I didn't lose a single job because I didn't have it. I was careful not to take on any risky jobs. I knew I was taking a risk. But it was a controlled risk.

But when they started this registration thing, I had to get it in order to get registered, and I needed to be registered to get any jobs.

# *Taxes*

If you are a sole proprietor, with or without a fictitious name, you file a Schedule C with your personal taxes.

EVERYTHING is deductible! When you buy a can of paint for your own living room, it's NOT deductible. But buy the same can for a gig, and it is.

You can deduct for the use of your car! You can keep track of your miles in a log. I use a second car primarily for the business, so I deduct the whole thing! I record my mileage every January 1st. Easy.

Don't listen to me for tax advice. I use TurboTax. They even figure out my self-employment tax.

I do file quarterly payments. Oh, you people with day jobs and W-2's! You have no idea how easy you have it!

# *How To Charge*

I like to charge by the hour, A. K. A. "time and materials".

I have a friend who is also a handyman. He charges by the job.

There are pros and cons to each method.

### By the job

My friend guesses how long it will take him to do a job, calculates how much he would like to make by the hour, and adds a fudge factor.

For example, it might take 3 hours to replace a vanity, sink, and faucet. He would like to make $30 an hour. So he figures 3 hours, plus 2 hours just in case something goes wrong. That's 5 hours, times $30, or $150. Add 20% in case something goes wrong (yes, he has two "in case" factors), or $30, for a $180 total. Then he rounds it up to $200, because anybody who will pay $180 would also pay $200.

That's just for the labor. Most people would like to pick out their own fixtures.

Yes, he added something extra twice. No! Thrice!

Yes, his bids are a little high. If it only takes him 2 hours, he's making $100 an hour.

Yes, he often doesn't get the job.

And you MUST factor that in! If he bids on five jobs and only gets one, and if he travels a half hour each way, then he's traveling TEN hours just making bids. Plus he has to travel to the job to do the job, plus spend those three hours doing the job. NOW what's his hourly rate? And how much gas can his truck burn in 12 hours?

People can buy a vanity, with faucet and sink, for under $200. It feels funny to spend more for installation than it cost to buy the thing.

The biggest problem a newbie has with bidding a job is that you have no idea how long a job will take.

- How long does it take to replace a mailbox post? What if you run into a problem, like blob of old cement that you can't get out?

- How long will it take to paint a room? You've painted many rooms in your life, but never with a stopwatch.

- How long does it take to replace a disposal? What if you have to go to the store for parts? Twice?

If you guess that a job will take 5 hours and it actually takes 10, you are not making $30 an hour, are you?

If you guess that a job will take 10 hours, and it actually takes 5, you will be charging so much that you won't be getting many jobs. So, I guess, it actually took you ZERO hours!

**By the hour**

I would tell that woman that I charge $35 an hour. I don't care if it's replacing a vanity or a mailbox post. Hell, I'll do your kid's homework for $35 an hour.

She will always ask, "How long will it take?"

The wrong answer is, "It will take as long as it takes." Another wrong answer is, "I have no idea."

You see, if you don't know how long it will take, she has NO IDEA! Her head is spinning. Is she writing a blank check? What if it takes 10 hours? 20? Is the sky the limit?

So I put a cap on it. I say, "It will probably take 3 hours, but we can limit it to 5 hours. So if it takes more than 5, then that's on me. But if it only takes 2, then you're only paying for what you use. So it could be as much as $175, but it will probably be more like $100, and it could be as low as $70.

I also point out that a real plumber would charge $35 per quarter hour plus a $100 service call. Yes, the real plumber is quicker, but that's not so important now, is it? Even if he could do it in a half hour, I'm cheaper. He's put $100 on the bill just by parking his truck in the driveway.

**An advantage to job bids**

People don't know what you make. Besides my handyman jobs, I like to build big swing sets and sheds. These are big ticket items, and I do charge a scheduled fee.

People don't know how much the lumber costs. They don't know how much labor is involved. They just look at the price and at the finished product, and see if it's worth it to them.

If I charged by the hour, they would see the cost of the lumber, and an hourly rate, which would be higher than my normal hourly rate.

For swing sets, they can look at similar sets at Toys-R-Us. My set is heavier, more substantial, and costs about the same as the store-bought set. Except the store-bought set comes in several boxes, and THEY have to put it together. Just getting the boxes home is a problem for some people. MY set is delivered! And assembled! For the same price as those boxes!

For sheds, they can see similar sheds at the big stores, and compare them to my shed. My shed is bigger, better, and cheaper.

The point is that they don't know your hourly rate. They can't say that you are not worth $35 and hour or that $35 is too high. They only see the bid. Is that new vanity worth $200 to them? Only $100?

## An advantage to the hourly method

Usually, while you're installing that vanity, the woman will say, "While you're at it, could you take a look at this kitchen cabinet door?"

My friend bid $200 for the vanity, so now is this woman is asking for some free work?

Should he say, "No problem, lady!"? Then he's working for free.

Should he say, "Sorry, lady, I'm only here to install the sink."? That won't keep her happy, and he would be turning down extra work.

Should he say, "OK, but that would be another $50."? Not a good way to keep your customer happy. And you are tipping your hand telling her how much you make per hour.

I have no problem with doing an extra job at my hourly rate. If she wants to add another job to the list, or TEN, I don't care. The clock keeps ticking.

It's typical. Once, when I was installing a new laundry tub, the woman added:

- Replace an old switch in her dining room with a dimmer switch,
- Install some weather stripping around her garage door,
- Adjust a bi-fold door.

None of these were especially complicated or time consuming, but they were not trivial, either. I bet they added another hour. What does that do to my friend's careful calculations?

And she knew she wasn't asking for anything free. She was just asking for a few more jobs to be done.

# How MUCH To Charge?

Don't expect to see THAT question answered here!

Rates vary around the country. And I bet rates vary between city and rural areas, too.

You should find out by asking a few other handymen. Go to your Pennysaver, and call them all. Ask how much it is for some made up job.

Let's take that vanity job again.

If they say, "We have a flat rate of $600" or "We have a flat rate of $100", then you know.

If they say, "We charge $90 per hour", or "We charge $20 per hour", then you know.

I hate it when they say; "I don't know lady. I'll have to come out and look at it." What would they have to look at? They've never seen a vanity before? They can't give you a ballpark?

They want to come out so they can apply more pressure. It's too easy for you to get the answer you want, hang up the phone, and never call back. It's harder for you to kick them out while they're standing there.

Well, if that's their game, then "Knock yourself out!" Make them make the trip, and see how they play you. They probably will start high, on a bid basis, and come down as they have to. But it will be easy for you to resist. Remember, you don't really want a vanity installed.

If your vanities are perfect, pick some other job. Find something hypothetical, yet typical. Something that doesn't require a visit. Ask how much to hang a ceiling fan, or wall mount a TV.

## Keep an eye on it

But that's only before you start your new career. It wouldn't be ethical for you to call him to the house of another handyman. What if he recognizes you?

You should keep track of your jobs. If people think you're charging too much, and you are losing jobs, maybe your prices ARE too high.

But if you NEVER lose a job, you are charging so little that people are taking advantage of you, that's not good either. Try cranking it up a little, then a little more, until you find that tipping point. You WANT to lose a FEW jobs.

## A Loop Hole

I have a friend in Australia. Here's something that is commonly done over there that I have never heard of over here. Yet as I show it to people, they don't blink an eye.

It's called the "Variations to Contract". Let's say they want you to replace a mailbox post. You guess it will take 2 hours, since you have to remove the old one, mix some concrete, etc.

But when you get into the job, you discover the old post has a blob of cement that will not move. It is jammed under the edge of the street pavement.

Now you have to go rent a jackhammer. It's another expense and another hour, and it's not your fault. Had you known about the blob, you would have taken it into account.

In my contract, if it's a bid contract, any variations to contract throw that old bid out the window. You can continue the job with the expanded parameters, but now the job switches to an hourly basis. Or you can quit now, half done, and let him continue with someone else, but he has to pay you for the time you already spent on the hourly basis.

If it's an hourly contract, it's not so traumatic. You just discard the upper limit. Either way, he's paying you by the hour. But now the job can go past the 5-hour limit.

(BTW – This DID happen to me. A blob of cement that I could not get out. But the answer is easy. Just pick another spot for the new mailbox! They loved it! The new mailbox was closer to their sidewalk!)

(BTW #2 – It doesn't take two hours. Because you don't have to dig a hole OR mix cement. See the tip in Part 4.)

**Fine Tuning**

Let's say a woman wants you to install a dimmer switch, and she lives an hour away.

Would you do such a very small job? What if it involves two hours of commuting round trip?

Would you turn it down?

Would you charge so much that NOBODY would want a dimmer switch installed at that price?

I have played with service calls (A. K. A., trip charges), and with minimum charges.

You could charge for the travel time. You could charge one hour minimum for the job, plus two hours travel. Now your price is high enough to keep you happy, but so high she could actually hurt your ear when she slams down the phone.

I tried charging a $25 service call. It turns out people expect it on plumbers and furnace jobs, but somehow they don't think we deserve it.

It's nice when you can get it, but when it pisses off a person so you lose a regular customer, it's not so nice anymore.

I play with my rate structure all the time. What works for me lately is a minimum number of hours. She understands that going that far for such a small job is unreasonable. So rather than paying $100 for a 5-minute job (she doesn't consider the travel time), she'd be more willing to pay $150 for three hours. So you're not charging $100 for a dimmer switch. You're charging $150 for a dimmer switch, and a ceiling fan, etc. And you don't mind driving an hour to get a three-hour job.

I base it on zip codes. In my own zip code, there is a one-hour minimum. One zip code out, it's two hours. Beyond that, it's three hours.

So ask, "Replacing that dimmer is pretty quick. Is there anything else on your list that would make my trip worthwhile?" Now if she wants to hire you for more jobs, everyone is happy. But if not, it wasn't YOU who said the job was too small.

And don't charge the service call, but I keep the service call on the work order, except I almost always waive it.

> "I always waive this service call, unless you are crabby. Crabby people have no idea that I waive it for everyone else. But YOU are not crabby. You are nice."

And then I strike a line through it. People love it!

## HomeAdvisor.com

This site says they tell you typical prices for typical jobs! How much should a homeowner charge for hanging a TV?

I heard an ad on the radio. I am to go to Pittsburgh.Homeadvisor.com

You should try your own city, or a nearby city.

Find their "True Cost Guide".

I looked up "Hire a handyman". Now, these guys do not go for the hourly cost basis. They assume you will bid the job.

Now, I'm not sure what the average job is. Six hours? Only two? Two days?

But they say the average cost was (as of this writing, in Pittsburgh) $392.

Then I am charging way too little! Or doing jobs that are too small!

Or maybe they are padding! This service is free to the customer. The handyman pays. So the handyman has to charge a little more in order to do this job. So maybe their jobs are all jobs done by their handymen, and therefore, are a little bloated.

Still, I charge $39 and hour, two hour minimum, plus a $25 trip fee. That's $103.

I used to charge $49 when I was starting out, and I got nowhere.

Maybe two hour minimum is too short? Maybe I should make it a THREE hour minimum.

They must be doing bigger jobs. Who would pay $400 to trim one hedge?

Then I looked at New York! If the average in Pittsburgh is $392, I wonder how high it is in New York!!!

Guess what! It's the same $392!

Did they just make up these numbers? Are these prices inflated so customers won't be shocked when their handyman hits them with a huge estimate? Which MUST be huge, to pay the home advisor commission???

# Loading Your Van / Truck / Car

Things were different when you were just "handy around the house."

Let's say you are in your own home, in your second floor bathroom, replacing a noisy exhaust fan. You decide you need your tin snips, and they are not in your tool belt. It's a bother, but you go downstairs, into your basement, and get them. You know exactly where they are, whether they're in a particular workbench drawer or hanging on the pegboard, so you don't waste a lot of time looking for them.

But now you're replacing someone ELSE'S fan. And you need those snips. Is it out in your car? Or is it back home? An hour away? Sometimes it's just better to go to the store and buy a new pair. You can put them with your other snips when you get back home.

I will not tell you how many duplicate tools I have.

OR, you could keep this new pair in your car. You learned a lesson.

It is a challenge to load every tool you will need, but not everything you own, into your car.

You also lose your workbench's organization. You know where those snips are in your workbench. It's another challenge to know where they are in your car.

**Lose an hour here, an hour there...**

Notice that you also LOST AN HOUR! Even if the store is only 20 minutes away! It's 20 minutes out, and 20 minutes back. Parking, walking into the store, finding the right aisle, choosing which pair you want, checking out, and walking back to the car HAS to add another 20 minutes.

But wait! It's worse! Did you leave your other tools scattered around while you were gone? You have to consider theft. You also have to consider safety. Will their kids be playing with your razor blade knife while you're gone? Will the woman be tripping over your extension cords? And if it's an outside job, you also have to consider the weather. So maybe you have to pack things up, and take things back out when you get back.

And THAT'S when you realize you also need your vice grips. Or your pry bar.

You see? Your first one-hour job could take four hours, and will make you wonder if this is your cup of tea. Stick with it; you will get better.

Before you go on your first gig, before you even advertise for your first gig, you should plan ahead and pack your car with the things you will need for your first job.

## My minivan

I have a Dodge Grand Caravan. It has a bigger "trunk" than the regular version. It has two side doors. It has a roof rack, which is good for ladders when I need them.

I did NOT go out and buy it. I'm using the old family car. We used to take vacations in it. Now it hauls tools and drywall. You do what you have to do.

## YOUR Car That You Already Have

If you have a 4-door sedan, you should see how long you can make do with it. Remember, this handyman career might not be right for you, and it would be silly to invest a lot of money on a vehicle. When you start out, you should use what you have.

I would remove the back seat (just the bench. It's easy.), giving you a bigger cavern to stow your storage boxes. And I'd take the golf clubs and everything else out of the trunk except the spare tire.

I just added a trailer hitch to my minivan. You could do the same to a sedan. It cost about $300 at U-Haul. Then I bought a used utility trailer from Craigslist. That was another $300. $600 is cheaper than a new car, and if the handyman thing doesn't work out, you can sell the trailer for the same $300, and you can always use your hitch for a boat. You could rent a trailer when your friends ask you to help them move.

## Vehicle of Choice

If I DID go out shopping, I'd buy a full-size van. A cargo van. A van I could stand up in, even if I had to crouch. I can't keep everything I need in my minivan. If I know I'll be doing plumbing, electrical, painting, or drywall, I throw in storage boxes dedicated to those jobs. But I don't have the room to carry everything I own all the time.

If I had a REAL van, I'd install shelving and organizers and keep more of the things I need occasionally.

I would NOT buy a pickup truck. I know they are the cool rage these days. But I keep a lot of tools in my van all the time. If I kept that much stuff in a pickup truck, it wouldn't be very long before I DIDN'T keep that much stuff, if you get my drift. I would have to buy a cap, but then my pickup truck wouldn't be so cool anymore. And how would you reach the deep stuff, up near the cab's window? There would be a lot of taking stuff out and putting stuff back.

## Organization

I have a system of storage bins. I keep 90% of the stuff I need in the van all the time. It is loaded as high as the windows, and there is about 2 feet of open space at the rear for the stuff I need occasionally. It is big enough for my power washer. It usually holds my bike.

I can put stuff on top of the storage bins. I can buy a sheet of drywall and put it inside. The tailgate does not close completely, but I can hold it down with a bungee. I can put occasional things on top, like my two-wheel hand truck or my compound miter saw.

Everything has its place. I don't waste any time looking for things. I can reach any box without removing other boxes. In fact, I can usually reach stuff out of a box without removing THAT box.

I put two 2x6 planks right behind the front seats. This keeps the boxes from creeping right up to the backs of the seats. That give me a nice place to put an umbrella, a briefcase, or a small bag of things I just bought.

At the left side door I have:

- My Tool Belt: Two screwdrivers (one of each, average size), three pliers, a pencil, a small tape measure, a razor blade knife, etc. Things that you use ALL the time.

- My main toolbox. Hammer, bigger tape measure, odd screwdrivers, volt meter, square, vice grips, tin snips, etc. Things that you less frequently than the things in the tool belt.

- A smaller toolbox for wrenches and sockets.

- A toolbox for my electric drill and everything it needs. Drill bits, socket adapters, screw driver tips, etc.

At the right side door I have:

- A bigger storage bin for odd stuff. Caulking gun, duct tape, hack saw, an empty Gator Ade bottle for emergencies, a radio, etc.

That consumes about 2 feet.

Behind that is my biggest storage bin. It's about as long as the van is wide. This holds most power tools, including a circular saw, a sawzall, a hammer drill, a dremel, and two extension cords on winder wheels. My rear seat belts stretch around this (with a bungee), so it doesn't become a projectile.

Behind that are two smaller bins, side by side.

- One contains clothing and other protective gear, like goggles, earplugs, and gloves. I have everything from shorts to sweatshirts. The weather can change. Some old people keep their houses VERY hot.

- The other contains nails and screws. I have smaller bins inside this one, organizing the many different sizes and types.

I also tuck in two old card tables, which are good for furniture assembly, and a step stool, which is good enough for curtain rods etc.

I can remove everything and reinstall the seats in ten minutes. And put it all back in ten minutes when I get home.

# *Documents*

When you go to your first gig, you should ask the lady to sign on the dotted line.

Shouldn't you bring along a dotted line?

## Work Order

You need a work order that specifies the jobs to be done and the cost. It should limit your liability, too.

For big jobs, work orders should also have a deposit amount, a start date, and a finish date. But my jobs are small. I'm in and out the same day. I get paid on the spot.

You need to get that lady to sign.

I can't imagine flying without it. I can't see doing a job just on the good faith of the customer. Imagine working for 3 hours, and telling her that the bill will be 3 hours at $35 an hour plus $25 service call, plus $75 for materials, or $205.

What if she objects to the $25? Or to the $35? Or to the 3 hours! Or even to the $75! It's too late now. And even if she pays, she'll want a receipt.

I have two work orders: one for bid jobs and one for hourly jobs.

You can download copies.

Go to:

> http://the-honey-do-man.com/book/work order bid.doc

and to:

> http://the-honey-do-man.com/book/work order hourly.doc

You should do these downloads now.

Open each document under word, and flip back and forth between this book and the documents using your task bar.

## You MUST make some changes

You must at least add your name, phone number, etc. But you should also make sure the rates are OK for your area.

If you do not have a computer, go get one. Or go to your library or Kinko's and ask for help. They can download these documents for you. They can even make the changes for you and print them out for you. Then you will have masters that you can copy.

Each document is a Word file. They don't say "HOURLY VERSION" or "BID VERSION", which would make the customer ask, "What's the other version?" You have to use your head a little. The hourly one has a detailed time log at the bottom. The bid one has a smaller time log, to be used only if the job becomes subject to "variations to contract".

For each document:

1. Add your logo or just type your name in a big font.

2. Add your zip code lists, or charge a flat fee for your trip charge.

   It looks like I charge a small service call fee for nearby zip codes, a larger fee for distances about a half hour away, and an even larger fee for one hour away. If it's more than that, I'm not interested.

   But like I said above, people get pissed at the service call. So I don't charge it. But it makes people feel good when I strike it out.

3. Put your name and address at the bottom.

4. Make any changes required by your state and local.

5. Print out a few of each.

### Filling One Out

Start with the date, name, address, etc. I file these forms. If a woman calls back after 6 months I don't have to ask her for her address again.

Write down the jobs that are to be done. I wish there was more room here, but the legal stuff just grew and grew. I'm trying to avoid two pages. The battle might be lost fairly soon.

### Warranty or As-Is

I warrant my work. To a point. There are some conditions.

Once I fixed a woman's washing machine, but I didn't connect one hose tightly enough. A week later it was leaking, and she called. I went back, and fixed it for free.

My friend has a cute phrase:
*"It's the least I could do. If I could have done less..."*

Of course, you would fix it for free, too. Imagine pulling out your contract, showing her the fine print, and either refusing to fix it or fixing it for extra money. Neither choice is a good one. Neither choice would stick. The ONLY choice is to fix it. For free.

All this legal stuff is wiggle room, for when it ISN'T my fault, or when the fix is too big to handle.

If a job is "as-is", it's not guaranteed. Say a pocket door is off its track, and you can't even see the track. Maybe you can remove some door trim and expose the track, and maybe you can put the little trolley back on its track. Or maybe you pull the trim and see the trolley is broken and you can't fix it at all. You couldn't have known that before pulling the trim. Or maybe one of the wheels came off the trolley and you were able to reattach it makeshift with a short screw, but you're not sure the fix will hold. That's "AS-IS". As-Is means you'll try your best, but there are no guarantees.

So let's say you begin work, and realize you can't fix it. Now what? You took off some trim, had your look, and reattached the trim. Did you mess up the trim? Do you have to caulk old nail holes? What about touch-up paint?

So you spent some time, so you should charge. But you didn't do any good, so you shouldn't. But your work wasn't guaranteed! So why not!!!

It's up to you, but in my experience, people won't pay. Or they will, and they'll never call you again. Even if you make them understand before you begin that the fix might not work, they don't really understand. It might be smartest to just walk away.

You can mark this box As-Is right away, before work begins. But many jobs BECOME As-Is, as you will see below.

### Labor Estimate (On the hourly form)

If you think a job should take 2 hours, write 3 or 4 as the PROBABLE number, and 6 or even 8 as the Maximum number, but remind them that if it only takes 1 or 2, that's all they'll pay for.

I often don't fill this in at all! People know that the job will take whatever it takes. If they authorize this job without the limit being filled in, then I can't be held to any limit.

Note also that if there is a variation to contract, the maximum no longer applies.

Note also that a variation to contract is ME finding some unforeseen situation, or HER adding something to the list! If I say a job will take a maximum of 4 hours, and she says, "While you are here, could you..." then how can I be bound to the old maximum?

### THE Most Important Part!

Of all the things to fill out, what's THE one thing you can't forget?

You have to ask the lady, "Could you please sign on the authorize line, so I can get started?"

Does that sound innocuous enough? If she won't authorize the work, you can't start, right? Obvious?

People never read this thing. Some even ask, "What am I signing?" Some start reading, but for some reason they quit. Maybe they fear that reading it would show a lack of trust. I have no idea. And I will never ask why they quit reading.

You could insert a clause that says, "I will pay you $100 if you say the magic word sassafras." You would NEVER have to pay.

After I do a few jobs for a woman, and it's clear she's not the cheating type, I don't bother making her sign anymore. Maybe that's another lesson I'm about to learn.

On the other hand, one woman stole my form! She signed it, and while I was working, it disappeared! So now I take the signed form back to my car while I'm going to get my tools.

**Variations To Contract**

Let's say you agree to replace a vanity for a fixed fee. When you pull the old vanity you discover that the floor is rotted, and it would be stupid (or impossible) to install a new vanity on a rotten floor. You could not have known this until you got into the job.

On the hourly form, nothing happens, except the maximum no longer applies. Ask the lady if you should fix the floor. If yes, the clock keeps on ticking. If no, then she should call a real carpenter to repair the floor and call you back, or maybe she decides she doesn't need a new vanity after all. Either way, you get paid for the work you did, and maybe again when she calls you back.

It's more complicated on the bid form. There are 4 ways to go, and it's on her to choose one:

1. Proceed. Install the vanity on the crappy floor. Do not enlarge the scope of the job to include repairing the floor.

   Stranger things have happened. Maybe she's trying to sell the house and doesn't care if the repair only lasts six months.

   This is the only choice that doesn't change the fee. You said you'd install the vanity, so install the vanity.

2. Stop the job: She decides that she doesn't want the vanity after all.

   Now you collect your hourly rate. You didn't do the complete job, so you shouldn't get your entire fixed rate fee. But you did spend some time. SHE'S the one who stopped the job.

   However, there are some jobs that CANNOT be left half done. Like a staircase without a handrail. If you say proceeding is not an option, it is not an option.

3. Suspend the job: She wants to think about it. Or she wants to wait until her husband comes home.

   In this circumstance I DO NOT waive my service call, since now you're making two trips. You have to put away your tools and take them out again, too. This job is now taking longer than you expected, and it's not your fault.

   In this case, I keep the work order open. I might return to finish the job. On the other hand, they might call you to say that they've changed their mind and don't want you to return. It could be difficult to get paid.

   Figure out how much you earned so far, and call it a deposit. So if they don't call back, you're good. If they do, then the work order continues and they've already paid something towards it.

4. Expand the scope. Fix the floor, then continue with the vanity. But the expanded work must be within your capabilities. What if the problem is termites, and you are not a licensed exterminator?

   But your original fixed bid only considered the vanity. Now you're ripping up old plywood, maybe even replacing a few joists, and so on.

## Warranty
I guarantee my work, but there are limits.

1. The customer has to declare the work is finished satisfactorily. This wiggle clause is especially slippery.

   There is a difference between you doing extra work because you're not finished yet, and coming back to do extra work on a job that WAS finished.

   Let's say you paint a room, and the lady says it needs a second coat. That's fine. The clock keeps ticking.

   But let's say you finish, go home, and the lady calls the next day and says she needs a second coat. Now you're painting that second coat for free, under your warranty.

   I did a job for a woman who was not home. When I was done, I left. When she got home, she decided she didn't like it and wanted me to come back. Now, had she been there, I could have fixed her problem on the spot and on the clock. Now it's an extra trip.

   Did you notice the "customer inspection" line at the bottom? Nobody else ever has either. The customer has to say the job is good. Nobody does. So no work is actually warranted. Like I said before, I will go back and fix a bad job. But if they treated me badly, they can't make me if I don't want to.

2. It has to be guaranteed at the outset.

3. Does not apply to "as-is" work. Yes, this is the same as number one, above, only backwards.

4. Does not apply to stopped work. Don't let me start building something, then stop me, then complain that I didn't finish it.

5. Does not apply to unpaid work orders. Don't let me do a job, refuse to pay, then complain that you want something fixed for free.

   One guy waited until I was done, and then complained that the price was too high. He would only pay me half. Fine. Just get me outa there. But then he called back that the work wasn't right. He wanted it fixed for free. I pointed out that there is no warranty for unpaid work. So he paid me the balance. And I STILL did not go back. Until he paid his late fee! HA!

6. May not apply if there are variations to contract. If there are any, I get to declare if the unforeseen conditions are serious enough to warrant going as-is. See the "becomes As-Is" box near the bottom?

7. For one year... A job won't haunt you for the rest of your life.

8. I will repair defects in workmanship (do a better job attaching that washer hose), or refund the labor charge. I could just refund their money. At least the labor part of it. Any materials I bought on the job are still theirs.

9. At MY discretion. I'll be the one to decide if I'll fix it or just send you a check.

10. There are no other warranties – standard legal talk.

11. No liability for consequential damages. I don't think this one will stick. If I install a banister, and it fails and causes your mother-in-law to fall, a judge might have a different opinion.

12. Warranty is for labor only. Once I installed a new microwave under a kitchen cabinet. I turned it on and it made a huge noise!

   The lady wanted me to remove it, take it to the store, bring her the replacement one, and install the new one. All for free.

   Why? Was it my fault? I felt bad for her, but it was NOT my fault. Maybe I should have compromised and done that extra work at half the rate.

## Payment

My jobs are so small that I don't ask for half down and half at completion. A deposit makes sense when you are spending thousands of dollars on a new game room.

I'm in and out the same day, usually in a few hours. I like to get paid at job completion.

Most of the time, they write me a check on the spot. They make it out to "The Honey-Do Man", and I deposit it into my checking account with that name.

Most people ask, "Who should I make this check out to?" They don't mind making it out to your own name.

Sometimes they pay cash.

But sometimes the person is not home when I finish. Or the person who will pay me is not at home. Or the wife wants the husband to check it out when he gets home. I expect them to mail me a check.

They usually do.

## Deadbeats

But rarely there is a problem. This is why you need the work order. You need something to take to the magistrate.

The fine print imposes:

- A $35 late fee, after 3 days. Plenty of time to write a check and pop it in the mail when they get home. NOT enough time to "get around to it."

- A $50 fee for stopped checks. If they get pissed and stop their check, they must really be pissed. It costs THEM money to stop a check. And it costs me money, too. My bank charges me when I deposit a check that doesn't stick. The deadbeat is also automatically in the $35 late fee territory by now, too.

- A $50 declined credit cards, and chargebacks. See the next section, below.

- After 30 days, I will go to the magistrate, and I charge the deadbeat an extra $100 for the trouble. And it IS a lot of trouble.

I have never actually charged any of these fees. If a person pays me a week late, I am happy to get the money, and I let it go.

I use these fees only to scare them. It usually works. I only had two problems:

## Deadbeat Number One

I once had an out-of-town guy who asked me to do several things. One task was to power wash his patio, which was bricks covered in moss. It took more than a day.

When I was done, he said it should have taken less time. And he wanted to pay me less. I think the time to negotiate is BEFORE the work gets done. Why do hookers take their money before they earn it? Because the value of the service diminishes after it's delivered. Or so I've been told.

We went back and forth in more than a dozen emails. I finally threatened him with going to the magistrate. I asked for all of those fees, except the $100 magistrate fee, which wasn't on the list at the time (another lesson learned). The magistrate adds his own court costs on top of that.

He finally did pay. You see, he KNEW he would lose. And there would be a judgment on his credit report. And he'd never be able to get a loan. THAT scared him. He paid in full before the court date. I withdrew the charges.

On this guy, I did NOT ask him to sign on the authorize line! ANOTHER lesson learned! With him being out of town, and with my never running into any problems with anybody else, I just didn't bother.

But through all these emails, he never realized that he never signed it! And I never had to prove it in court, although I could have. I think we had an adequate email trail, proving that he did ask me to do the work. Hell, he let me into his house. But NEVER AGAIN!

Here's what I shoulda-coulda-woulda done: Email him and attach his work order. It's already on your computer. Remember? You downloaded it and added your own changes. He can print out his attached copy, sign it, and return it with his deposit check. This is one exception to my deposit rule. The job would take 2 days, so 8 or 12 hours are significant, and makes a deposit seem reasonable. Also, he's out of town, so catching him is more difficult. Plus he's thinking about the deposit so he didn't even notice that he sent he the signed form.

OH! And take a picture of the check before you send it to the bank. I used to think that if the check was good I didn't need it anymore. And if it was bad, I would get it back. But if the deposit is good and you have trouble collecting the balance, his initial check has his account number, bank name, a real signature (not what he scribbled on your work order), and a good date. That's PROOF that he asked for your services.

## Deadbeat Number Two

A woman asked me to fix a bi-fold door. What happened is that she had some carpet installed, and now the door wouldn't clear the new carpet. She forced the door, and tore off a hinge. It was shot.

This bi-fold door only hid her washer and dryer. I suggested that maybe a vertical blind might be a cheaper, easier, and adequate solution.

We agreed that she would buy one or order one and I'd return to install it.

She asked me, "How much do I owe you for today?" I answered, "Let's let it ride. We'll settle up when I return." Another lesson learned.

She changed her mind. And she decided she didn't need my services after all.

I wanted my one-hour minimum and my service call. That's $35 + $25 = $60. I did go there, inspect the door, give my professional advice, removed the old door, hauled it to the garage so she could drag it to the street on trash day, and measured for the new one.

I phoned twice, and left messages. She never returned the call. Damned call screeners!

I wrote a letter, asking for my $60, plus the late fee, which I would waive if she paid the $60. She never responded to that letter.

So I wrote one more letter threatening the magistrate, and offering to waive again if she paid the $60.

And then I let it drop. This letter was only a threat. I had no intention of going to the magistrate for that little bit of money. If she pays, great. If she doesn't, let's move on.

Well, she finally responded! She never did pay, but she wrote me a big nasty letter about how I cheat old people.

And she wrote a big nasty letter to our Attorney General, charging me with all kinds of things. I answered it, and I think I'm done.

### Deadbeat Lessons

So, one deadbeat paid, one did not. And there were only two. Over five years. Maybe it wasn't worth the bother. But you can't let people walk all over you either.

The first deadbeat paid more than $300. It was worth it to me.

The second one only owed $60. Maybe I should have sent one billing letter and let it drop.

### Credit Cards

Some people want to pay via credit cards. You can refuse to accept credit cards, and you will be losing some business. But you won't be losing that much. Most people pay by check.

I have let people pay a little each month until they pay off their bill. I don't charge interest.

It's expensive to be able to accept credit cards. I did it for another business I used to have. I had to pay $50 a month whether I used it or not. Plus they took a cut of each sale. There is one flat fee per charge plus a percentage fee on the sale amount.

Most credit card merchants have a store, and they have a device on the checkout counter that scans cards. This proves they guy has the card.

My other business didn't have a store. I had an online business, where I was selling a book online.  There is more fraud on the Internet, because you don't have the actual card in hand. They charge you a larger cut when you can't scan the physical card.

For the handyman business, you could have a reader at your office. You could write down the credit card number and enter it when you got home. You don't have the credit card in hand, so you'll pay the higher cut.

I've seen ads for a new solution: You can stick this new gizmo into your sell phone, and now you can scan her credit card, while you're standing there in the lady's kitchen.

This is all quite a bother, and quite a hassle. And for very few sales, too.

Most people pay by check. A few pay in two or three checks over two or three months.

**It's easy to accept PayPal.**

If your customer is a member of PayPal, they can log in to their account, and send a payment to you. PayPal can suck money out of their credit card.

If they are NOT a member, PayPal can take a one-time payment from non-members without making them join.

To them, they're paying on a credit card. Maybe they'll pay your bill when their credit card statement arrives, or maybe they'll pay over time. It doesn't matter to you.

To you, it's cash, less a fee to PayPal. And PayPal doesn't charge $50 a month whether you use it or not.

So when they ask if you take credit cards, you just ask, "Do you have a computer?"

Sometimes, surprisingly, the answer is "No. I don't." Actually, you will be surprised when you see how many older people don't have one, and many of your customers will be older.

You could take down their credit card information, go home, and enter that info on their behalf, but that's a big no-no. You will be pretending to be them. That's fraud. You'll probably get away with it, but I wouldn't do it too often. If PayPal sees many different charges from many different customers all originating from your computer... I don't know if they are that smart. But they could be. And there's only one way to find out. So don't find out.

You can upgrade your PayPal account to a "Virtual Terminal", which makes it OK to enter their info at your home, but that ain't free.

If you have a PayPal account for when you buy stuff on eBay, that's not good enough. You need a merchant account. They have a limit on how much you can withdraw each month. You need to lift that limit.

There are two problems with PayPal:

1. You don't get your money right away. They hold it for 3 days.

2. They charge you 3%. I pass this on. I prefer a check. I can take a check and hold it until payday. If you MUST pay by credit card, it costs me 3%, which I pass on to you.

3. Yes, I said two problems. Chargebacks is a big enough problem that it earns its own section.

**Chargebacks**

With credit cards, you have to worry about chargebacks! If your customer gets pissed, they can call their bank and get that charge reversed. You have a chance to complain, but it's an uphill battle.

It's free to the customer. Stopping a check costs them, but asking the bank to start a chargeback is free.

If you use PayPal, you still have to worry about chargebacks. But now the chargeback is between them and PayPal. And then PayPal comes after you.

My policy is

> *"Pay your bill online and on time with PayPal"*

What's the point? What if a deadbeat pays my bill just to stop my action, then starts a chargeback to reverse that payment?

It hasn't come up yet, so I'm not sure if it will work.

And if he starts a chargeback, whether it works or not, DING! That's another fee in the late charge section of the work order.

# *Advertising*

## Cheap Advertising

What's cheap is NOT what costs less. The cheapest advertising pays for itself.

I was spending about $35 a WEEK on my Pennysaver ad. It was not pulling its weight. I let the contract run out.

I would spend $100 a week on other advertising, if it pulled in enough gigs to justify it.

## Tracking

You have to know where your leads come from. The next time you hear an 800 number on the radio, jot it down. Now find an ad for that same company in your Sunday paper. There is an 800 number there, too. Notice that they are different. Jot that one down too. If you're up late at night and see an infomercial for that company, it will have ANOTHER 800 number. They know which 800 number is getting all the calls. They know which ad is working.

You are not as big as these national companies. You will not get dozens of 800 numbers. You won't even get ONE! But there's a lesson to be learned here. You have to know where your leads are coming from. You have to know which ads are working.

Sometimes people will tell you. "I saw your sign on your car yesterday..." But that's not typical. Usually you have to ask. So ask. People will tell you.

## Too Cheap To Question

Some advertising is so cheap it doesn't matter how well it pulls.

Buy a box of business cards. Keep a few in your wallet, for when you bump into someone. Give one to every customer, even if you don't get that gig. Hand them out to cashiers and waitresses. It's like throwing sand at a wall. Some of it will stick.

I have pinned business cards to bulletin boards at a senior high-rise and at a grocery store.

I use MAGNETIC business cards! This story has happened a few times: A person sticks my magnetic card on their fridge. Then they sell the house, and the fridge stays. They're moving out of town, so they don't need me anymore. Then the new person moves in, needs some work, and sees my card.

A magnetic car sign is cheap, too.

## Val-Pack

This is a packet of ads that are sent to everyone. I tried this once. It got a few calls, and only one gig. It did not pay for itself. Maybe if my ad were better, or if I were better at closing a deal, the story would be different. Either way, I think this is not a good place for a beginner.

It's not very targeted. Out of a thousand packets, how many are tossed without being opened? And of those that are opened, how many people need a handyman? I mean, how many need one badly enough right then, urgently enough to actually pick up the phone and call?

You see? If the need were that urgent, they wouldn't wait for their Val-Pack.

What are the odds that you hit someone on that perfect day?

## Craigslist Is FREE!

Put your ad in the SERVICES / HOUSEHOLD section.

Your heading doesn't really matter. People won't start reading the listings page. Even if they do, in a day or two you will be pushed off page one anyway.

People do a search. The search looks in the body text, too.

Keep in mind how people search. Some people will search for
    "furniture assembly"
and some people will search for
    "assemble furniture".
You really should have both versions in your ad. But you don't have to say,
    "I love to assemble furniture. Don't do your own furniture assembly."
The words don't have to be together. You could say,
    "Furniture assembly is my specialty. I assemble swing sets, too."
The search WILL find "assemble furniture" since both words are in there.

But once they find a few ads, they will read them. So the body of the ad should be readable, too. You can't list a hundred jobs in your ad. It looks like you aren't a specialist in anything.

Imagine an ad that lists furniture assembly as the 20th item, right between gutter cleaning and power washing.

Now imagine another ad that talks only about furniture assembly. It mentions IKEA, Target, and OfficeMax, that you are cheaper than hiring the store for assembly, and how you can even pick it up at the store, and how you can come evenings and weekends.

And ALWAYS add some pictures!

So you should have SEVERAL ads, one for each specialty. And maybe one catchall ad for everything else.

And don't forget to keep renewing your ads. They expire in six weeks, but I don't wait that long. I delete and repost my ads every week. That keeps them near the top.

Also LOOK in the gigs section. This is where people place ads for work they want done.

**Jobs Fall Into Your Lap!**

You need a website. There's more on this in part 5, about marketing. You don't need it to assemble your first book shelf, but you will eventually need it.

But if you have one…

- A guy in Texas called me who manages rentals all over the country. He has me drive around to inspect a few local stores. I talk to the tenants, take a few pictures, and send him a repot.

- A guy in St. Louis called me who manages flag poles. But these are actually cell phone towers disguised as flag poles. They are more than 100 feet high. I have to change flags every six months and re-rope once a year.

- A guy in Rhode Island called me who does the maintenance for a half-dozen retail chains. The clerks who work at these stores don't know how to patch and paint, or fix a cabinet door.

# PART TWO

# Many Jobs You Can Do, And How To Upsell.

A woman calls you to install 2 mini blinds.

Is that all?

Was that worth the trip?

Wouldn't it be better to expand the job? Get her to authorize a few more jobs? Can you stay there a few more hours and earn a few more bucks?

## *I use "The Honey-Do Challenge."*

Tell the lady, "It's not worth my while to go that far to install two mini blinds. I have a three-hour minimum. Can you find me some other things to do while I'm there? I can't charge you $150 to install two mini blinds. But I CAN charge you $150 to do several jobs. Do you see? It's more worthwhile to me, and it's more worthwhile to you."

She has gotten so used to that rusty mailbox that she doesn't see it as a problem anymore. It's just a mailbox. It works. But her guests see it. It's just that none of them are rude enough to tell her about it. Ignorance IS bliss.

The lady will ALWAYS say, "I don't have anything else for you to do".

That's when you say…

> *"I bet you have had some problems so long that you have gotten used to them. But your guests see them; they're just too polite to tell you.*
>
> *I have never seen your house. You and I will walk through your house, and I will see problems that you no longer see. And I WILL be rude enough to tell you what I see.*
>
> *Between the two of us, we WILL find ten things.*
>
> *If we can't find ten things, I'll fix one thing for free!*
>
> *But if we CAN find ten things, what are you waiting for!!! Why are you living with these ten problems!!! You will probably fix them when you decide to move and sell your house. So why not fix them NOW, and YOU can be the one who enjoys these repairs!!!*
>
> *You can't lose! Either you get one thing fixed for free, or I can install those mini blinds and then do a few more jobs so you get your money's worth."*

**The First Loop Hole**

Don't worry. You won't be fixing a lot of things for free.

First, I KNOW I can find ten things. Sometimes I find ten things while we're still out in the front yard!

I am not limited to broken and rusty things. I am not limited to things I can fix myself. I can suggest a new driveway. I can't do that myself, but maybe I can sub it out. Besides, that's one more thing that I found.

I am allowed to suggest improvements. There's nothing wrong with that range hood, but wouldn't it be better to replace it with a microwave? Then you won't need that old microwave wasting space on your countertop. Why not replace that bedroom ceiling light fixture with a ceiling fan?

I am also allowed to suggest new things that add Pizzazz!

For example, look at the house numbers on your own house. If you have them, that is! Some people do not even have numbers. And do you know who needs them? Ambulance drivers!

You see? She did not see her house numbers as a problem, because she didn't have them! She didn't see them at all!

And if she DOES have them, I bet they're the standard black ones. They do serve the purpose. People CAN find your house if they are looking for it.

But there's no PIZAZZ! Imagine big brass numbers that draw your eye even if you're NOT looking for them!

Now you might not agree. You might not WANT to spend big bucks on brass numbers that you don't absolutely NEED.

But you found one thing that would improve her house. One down. Nine to go.

**The Second Loop Hole**

I usually find 20 or 30 things. Sometimes the owner stops the search after they realize there are plenty of things they have not been seeing.

And I STILL fix one thing! For FREE! I am such a HERO!

I get to pick that one thing. And it's always a little thing that requires no tools, no time, and no trip to the store.

Once I replaced a drawer front on a kitchen drawer. Four screws. Five minutes.

Once I put a bi-fold door back on its track.

What's the simplest and easiest job you will EVER find? I can't count the times I've found a ceiling fan going the wrong direction!

This is very dramatic:

- Notice that the fan is blowing upwards while it's even OFF! If the little switch is up, the air will flow up.

- Ask the woman to stand under the fan with you. Turn it on. Notice how little air you feel.

- While it's running, turn that switch. Don't bang your knuckles on the blades.

- The fan will slow, stop, and reverse. The motor will not burn out. That only happens if the motor can't turn. And it takes longer than one second.

- When it gets going again in the right direction, the effect is VERY dramatic!

Now, it's common knowledge that the fan should blow upwards in the winter, for better distribution of heated air, and down in the summer, so it blows on you.

This is not exactly correct. It should blow down on you when you feel warm and you WANT it to cool you, and there are times you feel warm in the winter.

Besides, that woman didn't even know about that switch. That fan was blowing upwards in the summer, too.

**Maintain The Right Attitude During The Challenge**

Remember that you are NOT actually throwing out a challenge.

You are NOT taking a chance with this challenge, and your main objective is not to dodge the bullet.

Your goal is NOT to find ten things so you can avoid fixing something for free.

You're trying to find things that you might be asked to fix:

- Things that annoy the owner.

- Things that no longer annoy the owner, because they got so used to them that they no longer see the problem.

- Things that don't annoy the owner because they never realized they had a problem. (But these things will annoy them now, now that they see the problem)

In other words, let's say you find some 2-pronged outlets.

Don't say, "HAH! That's EIGHT! This nightmare is almost over!"

Say, "You know, lady, those can be pretty inconvenient, and they're so easy to fix. Why don't you let me replace them for you? I don't have to replace every outlet in your house. Just the ones where you wish you had a three-prong one."

## Your Biggest Competitor

Who is your biggest competitor? Nobody!

That is, it's you, or it's nobody! They thought they wanted something done, but it's not an emergency, and pretty soon, the mood passes.

I once assembled a chest of drawers and a dresser for a woman. She said, "I couldn't stand stepping over those boxes anymore!" I asked, "How long have you had these boxes here?" And she said, "It's been FOUR YEARS!"

She thought she could do it herself, then she thought her out-of-town son could do it when he visited, etc. But when he visited, she'd rather spend the time visiting with him.

Most of these jobs are not critical. You can live with a kitchen cabinet door that is off on one hinge... You just have to be careful when you open it. You can live with a laundry tub that drips... how much water can it be wasting?

"I'll get around to it" is your biggest competitor. Maybe your business cards should look like this:

There. Quit saying you'll get "around to it." Now you have "a round tuit."


## My Challenge Form

You can download a copy at:
http://the-honey-do-man.com/book/challenge.doc

It's a Word document. The downloaded version fits on one page. Add your name and phone number at the top, and print out a few copies.

Don't forget your phone number! When you're done, you will leave this sheet with your customer. They might set it aside, look at it later, and it would be a real shame if they had no way to call you.

Each item has a check box. You mark a check if there is ANYTHING wrong with the item. You check it if the item is MISSING! And you check it if it's fine but could be improved with some PIZZAZZ!

For example, the first item is the mailbox.

First, if it's rusty, if the flag is missing, if the door only has one hinge (I've seen them all), you should check it.

But if it's fine, you can STILL check it. Why not replace it with one of those big baseball-bat-proof ones? Those ones even have a newspaper hole. This is a big advantage if their newspaper is always in the driveway, sometimes in the rain. And some of them have a smaller back door. You don't have to step into a busy street to get your mail. This is a plus if you have your smallish kids get the mail.

Does it have numbers? Maybe they have their house number on the house. But house numbers on the mailbox or mailbox post are better. Most house numbers can't be seen in the dark. Mailbox numbers will have headlights shining on them. Ask any ambulance driver.

And it doesn't mean you have to remove the ones on the house.

You want to sell this person on a new mailbox. Show them the problems with the old one, and show them the benefits of a newer, bigger, better one.

## Repeat Business

Getting one visit to last a little longer is nice.

But coming back for another visit, and another, is much nicer.

Marketing experts agree that it's easier to get repeat business out of an old customer than it is to get a new customer.

If you did a nice job, if you didn't charge an arm and a leg, if you didn't track mud into her house, and if you didn't teach her toddler any new words, then she will call you back.

Sometimes they ask, "While you're here, could you fix this hinge?"

And you can say, "Of COURSE I can fix that hinge. But I have to go get one first. How about I take that broken hinge with me so I can match it, and I'll bring a new one the next time I come back."

OK, maybe that was a little extreme, keeping her hinge hostage, but you get the idea.

But the whole idea of the challenge is to find more things for you to do. You might do a small one while you are there, but more often than not, it results in a repeat visit.

## Call People Back

I keep all my old work orders on file, in LIVE, WARM, and COLD folders.

The LIVE folder has between five and ten work orders. These are jobs that I'm scheduled to do in the next few days, and jobs where I'm not done and have to go back to finish.

The WARM folder has jobs I've recently completed. I can call these people back in two weeks or a month and try to scare up some new business. "Did you go buy that ceiling fan yet? I have an opening this week."

Maybe she says she didn't get around to it yet, so there's some hope. Or maybe you get the feeling that your mission is complete at this house.

The COLD folder holds old jobs where I'm NOT going back. There's no imminent work scheduled. I can call these people back in six months, or even a year.

Sometimes these people call ME! I always leave them with a magnetic business card. When the need arises, they can call.

I can look up their old work order and have their address, maybe an extra phone number than what they called in on, and a reminder to me of what jobs I did there.

**One Cheesy Trick**

As you leave a job, jot down some personal info on their sheet. The kids' name is Sammy, the lady was about to take a cruise, etc.

When you call back a person in the WARM file, you could say, "So how was your cruise?" or "How did Sammy do on his math test?"

They will be surprised how you took such an interest in their life. You are no mere handyman. You are a true friend.

When a COLD person calls, you won't have their sheet in hand. But when you show up, you will be armed with this info.

**So let's get to it!**

As you read through this list, BE AMAZED at how many jobs there are that you, the average handy-around-the-house guy, can do!

I bet you can do ALL of these jobs. I bet you HAVE done most of them. But I bet you never made a list before.

And I have done almost every one of these jobs for pay. As simple as many of these jobs are, there are people out there who will pay.

And as you read through this list, let's both walk through YOUR house, in your mind. How are YOU doing? How many things might I find at YOUR house!!! And if I can find that many things at YOUR house, a self-professed handyman, imagine how many things you might find at someone else's house.

Go get a beer. This is a long list.

If you are reading this book online, open the Honey-Do Challenge form now. Then you can flip back and forth between it and this book using the task bar. People with the print version should download it and print one out.

# *Outside*

## Mailbox

See above. Except for one good tip:

You don't need to dig a hole, mix some concrete, then clean up the mess after your wheelbarrow spills, etc.

Wait until you see the tip in Part 4, below.

## Railing

Missing? Some local codes require them if there are more than 4 steps. Emphasize liability. Emphasize ice and snow.

Rusty? An EXCELLENT example of a problem that they no longer see.

Consider a new vinyl one. They are not difficult.

## Walk

Cracks? You can fix a crack.

Do they have paver stones that are sinking and are getting covered with grass? Do these sunken pavers collect water? Do they have to walk through puddles? Do they have to walk on ICE???

There is no need to dig out the old ones. Just place a NEW layer of pavers over the old ones!

## Steps

Broken? Slanting so they would be downhill when icy?

## Flag pole

For the American flag. Or for fun flags.

It can be a small pole attached to the house or a tall pole erected in the front yard.

Almost EVERYBODY gets this check.

It doesn't matter if they don't want a flag. You suggested it. It's a check.

### Bushes

Overgrown? People tend to trim bushes infrequently. So they take off only a little. And they tend to grow bigger over time. Finally, they block windows.

They also trim them so a big bush only has one or two inches of green. Inside that green shell, it's just sticks.

The best thing to do is to saw them off at ground level. No need to get the roots. Then plant new bushes, only one or two feet tall. Add a few bags of mulch, and you won't believe the difference.

### Trees

You can trim low branches that make it difficult to cut the lawn.

Overgrown trees? Too close to the house so the roots become a problem?

This is a job for a professional if power lines are involved, or if the trees are HUGE!

But many trees are no big deal. If you can put an extension ladder on it, you can do it.

Take it down in pieces. Lop off the top, lop off the big branches, and finally take down the trunk in pieces.

You can rent a stump grinder. But if you tell the lady that this step is optional, and extra, she'll admit that she wanted the tree out of there but that she really doesn't care about the stump.

Did you know there are stump removal chemicals? You chop the top of the stump with an ax, sprinkle on this chemical, and the stump rots.

### Numbers

Are they missing? Are they visible from the street? At night?

I was at a housing development once where every house had the same porch light and every house had the same style of numbers. And the porch light did NOT light up the numbers. Pray that your heart attack happens in the day time.

This is a perfect item for Pizzazz.

## Doorbell

Does the doorbell work? Does it work only sometimes?

It's usually the button. And the problem is that the contacts are all corroded. It's easy to fix. Just take it out, sand the wires, and put it back. This could be your free thing!

I did make one mistake once… I opened the doorbell button, touched the two wires together to see if that was the problem, and it was! The doorbell rang! And I lost a job! Now they knew what the problem was as well as I did. They didn't need me.

A new button is less than 5 bucks, takes less than 10 minutes, and the new button even lights up! Carry one or two with you. If I had a button with me on "mistake day", I could have attached a new button, then tested it, and then proclaim, "I fixed it!" Now it doesn't matter if "now they know". It's too late for me to unfix it.

Do they even have a doorbell?

Now they have remote ones! You don't need to run a wire from the button to the basement, or from the basement to the chimes.

It's easy to install the button outside with two screws.

There are two kinds of chimes. Battery and plug in. The plug in one is best. It doesn't have to be at the front door. It can be in the kitchen, or any other place where the family usually is.

It's not hard to run a new wire from a new button to the transformer in the basement. IF there is a screen door, you can remove the trim strip opposite the hinge. You can drill a diagonal hole into the basement. Then replace the trim strip.

## Peep hole

Most people can use one. Most people don't have one.

They're easy to install, and cheap too.

Maybe you could stock a few in your car, and THIS could be the one thing you do for free.

Maybe they'll decline. They really don't want one. Hey, you offered! Obligation satisfied! One more checkmark.

BTW, did you know there's a song about peep holes?

> *Peep hole,*
> *Peep hole who need peep hole,*
> *Are the luckiest peep hole in the world.*

### Door

This means the entry door AND the storm door.

Did you ever see that guy who wears a nice suit and really cares about his appearance? But then he drags out this ratty old wallet that's falling apart and is held together with an old rubber band, because nobody sees his wallet!

The same thing applies to front doors. People don't see their crappy front door.

If it's old, it also leaks.

I remember a story about one door salesman. He would ask the prospect for a $5 bill. He would slip it under the closed door.

He says, "You see? If a $5 bill could get through there, then your warm air is getting through there all the time!"

And the client says, "Right. I get it. Let me open the door and get that $5 before it blows away."

And the zinger: "What? You care about that $5 because you can touch it? But you don't care about the other $5 bills you lose all the time because you can pretend they don't exist???"

And the salesman blocks the door, as the owner gets more and more anxious.

And many people don't have a storm door. They are good in the summer with the screen in. They are an extra layer of insulation in the winter.

And many existing screen doors are crap. They were crap when they were new. And you should see them now.

Does the closer close the door? Or slam it?

And don't forget the back door. And maybe a basement entrance door, too.

You can repair a screen, too. In the winter, ask to see the screen, which is stored in the basement.

See part 3.

### Gutters

Almost everyone's gutters are clogged. Even if the homeowner gets up there every month, they are probably clogged again a few weeks later. And NOBODY bothers to snake the downspouts.

Sometimes you can see tree sprouts! If you fill a trough with mulch, wet it, and lay a maple seed on it, what do you think happens?

"Oh Look! PLANTERS!"

Gutters that don't work are like having no gutters at all. And all that roof water can undermine the foundation. It's easier to scoop out the gutters than it is to repair a bad foundation.

The easiest way to clear gutters? A leaf blower!

But you should also snake out the downspouts, too. All you need is one of those hand crank versions.

Gutter Helmets? They make icicles! And when the little holes clog up, they don't work.

I upsell with Gutter Fillers! It's a long porous sponge that fills the gutter. How can the gutter fill with leaves if it's already full with this filler? Leaves just lie on top, dry out, and blow away.

## Pool

I don't do pools. But maybe you like this job. If you do, it's a recurring job.

But is there a fence? Installing a fence is better than finding a dead kid at the bottom. Most places require a fence, and they probably have one. But is it in good repair?

## Power wash

Talking about pools... Is there a deck? Could it use a good cleaning?

Paved driveways need it too. You don't THINK it needs it, but when you're done, WOW!

Do you see moss? Some people see green and assume mold. Mold is scary. Don't correct them. Just point out the green.

Power washing can get chalk and even paint off a driveway. Or a brick wall. It can remove graffiti.

If you have one, you can always suggest something that could stand a good cleaning. "After I'm done with your porch, why don't I hit your lawn furniture?"

If you don't have one, get one. It will pay for itself.

## Shed

Do they have one? If not, that's a big-ticket item. You can build one, or you can assemble a kit.

They have so much junk in their garage they can't get their car in.

Remember that old saying? "Sears doesn't sell drills. They sell holes."

You're not selling a shed. You're selling them getting their car back in their garage. They won't have to scrape snow from the windshield. They won't have to get in a hot car.

And if they DO have a shed, I bet it needs work. Sheds are more neglected than houses. Some have raggedy edges from rot. It's not hard to replace the skin with new plywood. It's even easier to apply a trim board along the bottom. Just cover that raggedy edge.

And if it's not that shot, maybe a new coat of paint will be enough.

Now look inside. How efficiently are they using their space?

Hang pegboard on the doors!

Turn around and look above the door. Is there room for a shelf above the door? This space is always wasted.

Is there a loft shelf? I have seen shelves only big enough to hold a row of paint cans. A loft shelf is almost a 4x8 sheet of plywood, about 3 feet high. If they put the lawn mower in, is there anything above the lawn mower? Are they wasting all those vertical cubic feet? I can put my lawn mower under my loft shelf and then put two rows of boxes above my lawn mower.

And how are they using their space OUTSIDE! Why not hang the wheelbarrow on the shed's outside back wall?

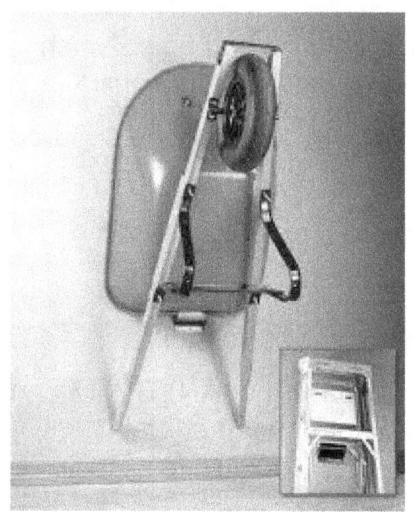

This picture is in a garage, but you get the idea.

You can hang ladders outside, too. Contractors store ladders and wheelbarrows on their trucks, which always stay outside.

Do they have a canoe? Hang IT on the shed, too!

Ding. I can find ten checkmarks in a SHED! And if I have to organize it, toss junk, install a shelf and some hooks, etc., we're easily up to three or four hours.

### Locker

Maybe they don't need a shed. Maybe a vinyl storage locker would be enough storage. Rubbermaid and others make lockers that are four or five feet wide and four feet high. Keep it on the back porch and now you have a place for your gardening tools. Maybe even your lawn mower. Take it with you when you move.

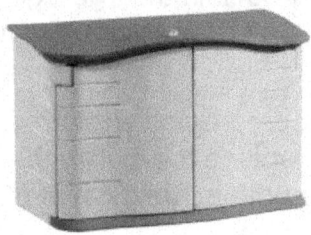

### Fence

Installing a new fence is harder than you might think. It's not a job to try your first time on someone else's house.

But if there's a broken section, or if it needs paint, or if the latch doesn't line up, go for it!

### Porch

Is it under cover? Then it's dirty.

If it's not under cover, why not? Sitting on your porch in the shade is very Norman Rockwell. (If you don't know who that is, ask your dad).

Maybe it needs paint.

I've seen ratty indoor-outdoor carpet. People will do this to cover a bad finish, such as chipping concrete or peeling paint. And now the carpet is bad. And it's stuck down with glue.

### Lights

Does the front porch light work? The driveway light? IS there a driveway light?

Are they rusty?

How about the walk? And the steps? Are they dark? You can get solar lights.

They won't hire you to go get the solar lights. That job is so easy that ANYBODY can do it. If they do it at all, they'll do it themselves, after you pointed it out to them.

But it's another checkmark.

### Trashcans

Are they hidden behind some bushes? It's not cool to see them out in the open.

Maybe you could build a little hidey-hole with two sections of fence.

## Lawn

Does it need to be cut?

Is it hard to cut? Is there a lot of trimming to do? Did they cut the grass, but is it still long on the edges? You can install a better border around the edges. Rows of bricks or mulch can eliminate trimming.

The lawnmower wheel rides along these low bricks. NO trimming. This looks good, too.

Does the lawn need to be replaced? Does it have to be replaced with another lawn? Maybe a bigger driveway would be better, accommodating more cars, and eliminating some lawn.

## Leaves

Is it time to blow leaves? A perfect job for you. An impossible job for an old lady.

One older lady said that she asks her son to do it when he comes to visit. But when he does come, she'd rather spend that time visiting with him.

## Driveway

Cracks? You can fix small cracks with a caulk gun and a tube of repair stuff.

Stains? Power wash!

## Walls

Are the retaining walls leaning? They don't fix themselves.

> *"You better get your car out of the garage before that wall falls and blocks you in."*

## Roof

Are there missing shingles? You can replace a few missing shingles.

A new roof might be beyond your capabilities.

## Windows

Are they old aluminum, single pane, I mean, single "pain"?

Are they even older wooden ones?

Replacing a window is a job that might scare you, but it is possible. It might take you four hours to do your first one. But you will get better.

## Awnings And Gazebos

IS there an awning? I like sitting in the shade much better than sitting in the sun. But some people like to sit in the sun. They like to get a nice bronze color as they nurture their self-inflicted case of skin cancer. But to each his own.

Canvas awnings should be taken down for the winter. This goes for gazebos, too.

You just take down the canvas and the screens. The frame stays up. And WHO do you think she'll call in the spring?

Why not suggest a retractable, maybe even motorized, awning?

### Deck

Is there a deck? What's its condition? How dirty is it?

## Take a Break!

That's the end of the first section. We are not even halfway down the first column! We're still outside. If you don't have ten checks by now, you're just not trying!

Go get another beer.

Holds Cans
Or Bottles!

# *Main Living Area*

There are only ten topics here, but they each apply to the living room, dining room, family room, and hall (entrance hall, bedroom hall, etc.) So that's FORTY boxes to check. Unless they also have a den, and a library, and an office, and a hobby room...

I once had a woman who had a stamp room. A stamp room? What's that? Turns out she had a hobby of stamping paper with her collection of rubber stamps! She had stamps for butterflies, flags, etc. She would sit there and fill a whole sheet with butterflies! Or bunnies! Sounds a little first-grade to me, but to each his own. And she had a whole room dedicated to this!

### 2-prong outlets

Older houses have 2-pronged outlets. Some people get by with an adapter (they plug into the 2-prong outlet, and provide three holes to plug the device into).

The problem is that you're supposed to ground it! You're supposed to put the faceplate screw through that small loop.

NOBODY BOTHERS! I unplug the device, hold the three-prong plug up to the woman, and ask, "Would you ever cut off this third prong?"

They always, say, often indignantly, "Of course not! I would NEVER do that!"

"Well, that's exactly what you're doing when you fail to ground the adapter."

I taught this same lesson to one woman TWICE! It does not sink in.

You should get a tester. It has three prongs, and three lights. You plug it in, and it detects the most common problems that most people make (reversed hot and neutral, open ground, etc.)

Show the woman how her third prong is flapping in the wind.

This could be your FREE item: Remove the faceplate screw, install the adapter correctly, and test again. Poifect!

Now, this only works if the BOX is grounded. If the correctly installed adapter doesn't test, you'd be doing her a favor by throwing her adapter away for her. (no, this wouldn't count as your free thing!)

But if the box IS grounded, you just found yourself one of the easiest jobs there is. You can install a new, three-prong outlet, and IT WILL TEST!

Replacing a 2-prong outlet with a 3-prong outlet costs about a dollar and about 15 minutes.

**Too Many Plugs**

If you see this                                        Then you can suggest this

                 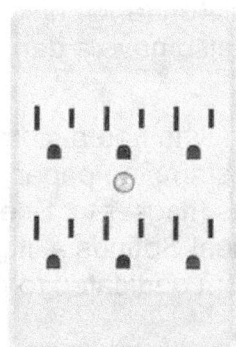

It's just as many things plugged in, but it's neater.

BTW, it's not how many things are plugged in; it's how many things are turned on at the same time. Remember Ralphie? In The Christmas Story? "You'll shoot your eye out!"  "A quick whiff of ozone..."  Now THAT'S too many!

Look behind the TV.

I bet you DO see six things plugged into one outlet. There HAS to be a TV, a VCR, a cable box, a DVD player, and there's probably a game console and a lamp.

Do you see a surge protector? People put these near their computers. But hardly anybody thinks to put one at their TV. And the TV costs more than the computer.

Now, nobody will hire a handyman to install a surge protector. But it shows you are primarily interested in their well-being.

And these things are SO CHEAP, you could offer to give her one FOR FREE! (on your next visit, of course!)

This package has a surge protector PLUS another strip that's NOT a surge protector, but it's good for untangling a nest of wires. LESS than $10!

### Drape rods

Never use a plastic drywall plug. Always try to drill into solid wood.

And there's ALWAYS wood right there! Imagine the wall when it was being constructed! There is a stud there, and one layer of drywall. You KNOW where the wood is without a stud finder.

Oh yeah, buy a stud finder, too.

### Drapes

If there are drapes, they are OLD drapes. This is something they got used to.

Maybe mini blinds or vertical blinds would work better.

## Doors

Check every door. Does it close? Does it open? Or is it warped or swollen so you have to force it.

Does it drag across carpeting? Sometimes people add carpeting and fail to trim the bottom of the door.

I open the door until it's pushing on the carpet at the worst spot. Then I lay a pencil on the carpet and draw a line on the door. The angle of the pencil point is perfect. Then take the door outside, saw it with your circular saw, and reinstall.

Be careful that you are sawing the BOTTOM of the door! You can cut some off the top and it will still hit the carpet on the bottom. Stranger things have happened.

To remove a hinge pin, some people use a screwdriver and a hammer and attack that top button. This is wrong. You should use an ice pick (ask your grandfather) and a hammer to push that pin up from below. Then grab the shaft with your needle nose pliers, and hit the pliers with the hammer.

## Door knobs

Does the latch snap? Does it lock? Before you chisel the latch hole, step back and see if the door is out of alignment.

Imagine the door twisted counterclockwise. It will be tight on the left side at the top, on the right side on the bottom, and on the top at the right side.

The problem is NOT the latch.

You may be able to fix this problem by inserting a piece of cardboard behind the top hinge.

Even if the doorknobs are perfect, maybe the new lever ones would be better! They are good for people with arthritis. They are also good for people with their hands full. You can carry a baby and a diaper bag and still open the door with your elbow.

## Shelves

EVERYBODY can use more shelves. If there is clutter, then they need more.

They can buy new ones, and you can assemble them.

Or THEY can assemble them (it isn't hard), but you still get to make one more check mark.

## Entertainment center

Many people bought huge entertainment centers. They have room at the top for a TV, doors to hide the TV, and a section below for the stereo.

Then they bought a new flat screen TV that doesn't fit in that hole!

You can find these old entertainment centers on the free section of craig's list all the time. Some under "Curb alert".

They need a new unit that is shorter. The TV sits on top, and is not confined to a small hole.

OR...

Be bold and suggest a TV wall mount. Most mortals dare not try this. But it isn't too hard. See part three.

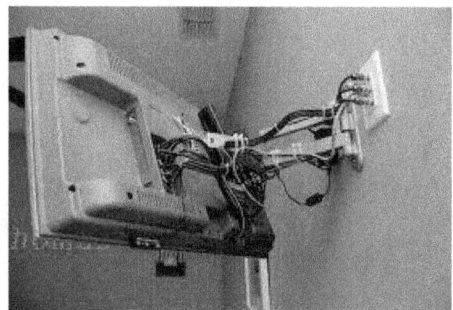

# *Kitchen*

### Cabinets

One woman complained that one cabinet door would not stay closed. She used it every day, for drinking glasses. The springs were shot.

I swapped hinges with a door that she rarely used. It was a small door above the fridge where she stored her once-a-year things.

Maybe THAT'S your free thing!

I have hung new cabinets in two kitchens. It's a big job.

I would not attempt it without a "Third Hand", a very cool tool. See the tip in Part 4.

### Ceiling Fan

They are more common in bedrooms, but why not have one in the kitchen? Don't you get hot in the kitchen?

You might be tempted to get a small one. But I bet the full-sized 52" one would work just fine. It's higher that the fridge door, right?

### Microwave

You can hang a microwave under a cabinet, and free up some valuable counter space.

You need a microwave that is designed for this; you can't mount the one that's on the counter. She wants a new one anyway.

And you need a rather short cabinet, too. Imagine a microwave hanging so low that there's no room on the stove for a pot.

But if you see a range hood, you are in business! You already have a short cabinet, and you already have power, and you even have an exhaust vent.

### Other Under-Cabinet Things

There are other under-cabinet appliances, too. There are coffee makers, toaster ovens, can openers, radios, and TV's.

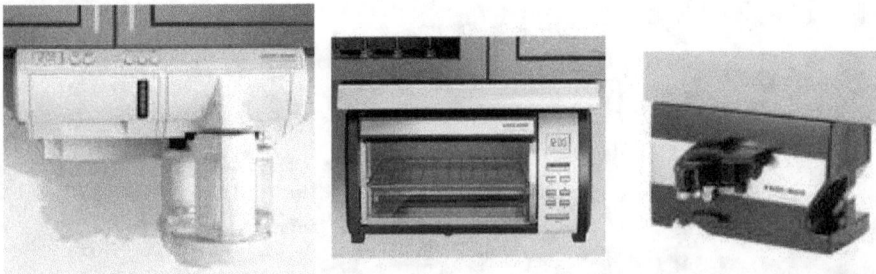

And don't forget under cabinet lighting! It won't save any counter space like the others, but look!

How about these! Keep your cookbooks out of the slop, and classy glasses.

### Disposal

This one could be tricky. It's not too bad if you're replacing a bad one.

It's a little harder if you're installing the first one. You need power. And a switch. And you need to redesign the drainpipes.

One guy called, and asked me if I could install one. I asked if he already bought one.

He said, "Yep. I got the permits, too!"

PERMITS? I passed on this job. You see, if he's in the city, and he got permits, then the job will be inspected. This guy hung himself. Now he needs to hire a real electrician and a real plumber. And I am neither. Or maybe he should keep his mouth shut while he's talking to the next handyman.

### Icemaker

This one's easy. I've replaced a bad icemaker.

I've installed icemakers where there was none. Just be careful that the fridge is ready for one.

I have even seen fridges that had an icemaker that was not hooked up to a water line!

And think about where you will get your water supply. If the sink is nearby you can go through a cabinet wall. Otherwise, you have to go to the basement. Hope that the floor is not ceramic, and hope that there's a pipe nearby.

## Fridge doors

It's amazing how many people tolerate backwards fridge doors.

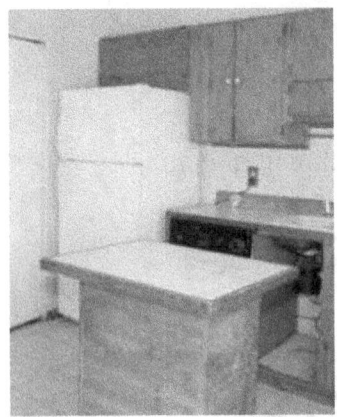

This fridge is at the left end of a counter, and its doors are WRONG!

It would be so nice to open the door, get a few things out and set them on the counter, and close the door.

On shopping day, it would be nice to put several things on the counter, open the door once, and put everything in.

But you have to walk past this fridge! And the open door blocks the counter!

Now imagine it with the hinge on the left, opening towards the counter. Heaven.

Almost all fridge doors can be swapped. Except for a side-by-side one, which, IMHO, is always wrong!

- The top hinge comes off, and the freezer door stays in place because of the magnetic gasket.

- You can lift off the door without emptying the shelves.

- The handle comes off, unless it has no handles. Some have an indent on the edge of the door. These have TWO indents, one on each side.

- Notice the holes at the top. They can hold either the hinge or the handle.

- Then it's the same with the lower door.

There was one fridge that gave me trouble. It had ice and water through the door. The plumbing did not reverse. This door was not designed for switching, but it looked like it was because they used standard doors used on other models. I shoulda read the manual. But nobody ever reads those things!

## Pantry

Is there a pantry? Is it well organized? Does it have efficient shelving? Or can it only hold some boxes of cereal and a couple of mops?

And what if there isn't one? MAKE ONE! Is there a doorway to the cellar? You can buy a wire shelf that attaches to the door with 4 or 5 shelves. You don't see it unless you open the door.

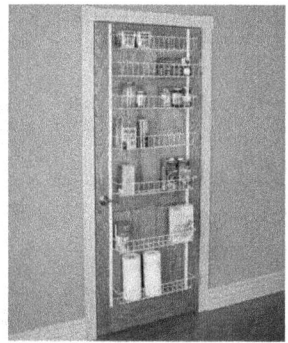

Sorry, but this is the best picture I could find. It looks like it's on the outside of a bedroom door. But I guess they were primarily interested in the picture.

If this were the steps to the basement, or to a broom closet, you would put the rack on the inside. But that would make a crappy picture.

## Countertop

Look for clutter, and suggest some storage solutions.

Old countertops can be replaced. Sometimes a seam separates, and water makes it swell. That cannot be fixed. They need a new one.

If they want another formica one, that's a possible job.

But if they want granite, you should sub it out to a pro.

## GFI

All outlets near water must be Ground Fault Interrupters. Those are the outlets with the test and reset buttons. They kill current much faster than a circuit breaker.

They are easy to install. The white, black and ground wires are obvious.

But did you know that if there are three outlets, you may not need three GFI's? If power comes to the first outlet, and then daisy-chains to the second and then to the third, you only need one GFI at the first outlet.

It's not hard to determine which is the first outlet. Disconnect everything, and find the hot wire with your tester.

When you're done, hit the test button on the GFI, and make sure that the other two outlets go dead.

There are GFI's that go in the breaker box, too. Everything on that circuit is protected.

An outlet might be GFI protected even if you don't see any test and reset buttons.

You need GFI's in the bathroom, and outside too.

We'll catch that bathroom one later on our tour.

But it looks like we missed that outside one. Hey, we're not doing a thorough home inspection here. We're just trying to drum up business.

## Take Another Break!

That's the end of the first column! Time for another beer.

BTW, did you know that you don't hold a stein like a normal mug? The lid will hit your ear, as if it were about to slice it off. You hold the handle away from your face, so the lid almost touches your forehead.

Lucky this is your day off!

# *Basement*

## Shelving

Could you install new shelving and get some clutter up off the floor?

Did you know you could put a shelving unit in front of an identical unit? It's like a shelf that's twice as deep. Without using any extra wall space, now you have double the shelving. And if you put a Christmas box behind another Christmas box, you don't even have things hiding other things.

Don't put the diagonal bracing behind the front unit. But you CAN connect the two units together.

## Clean out

Is the clutter worthless junk that's not worth putting up on shelves? Is it time to toss some stuff?

Here's the best way to clean out a basement: You clean my basement, and I'll clean yours.

I am not attached to your crap. There is no sentimental value to me. If it's so bad that I couldn't even sell it on ebay, it's gone.

You could be the better person to clean out that basement. But so far, not one customer has agreed with me.

When you clean out a basement, you don't HAVE to throw EVERYTHING out! You can keep the good stuff. And by good, I mean things that could sell on craigs list or on eBay. And you can sell a three-legged table on eBay.

## Laundry

There should be a shelf above the washer. A big jug of detergent should sit on that shelf.

At my own house, I built a small holder from scrap wood, so the jug is tipped.

When should you open that upper cap for air flow? If it's tipped, wouldn't some detergent come out if you open it too soon? I poke an air hole in the jug on day one, at the highest point after the jug is tipped. I NEVER open that vent cap.

There should be a rod above the dryer, for hangers.

Some houses don't have vents to the outside! They make do with a filter that is ALWAYS full! You CAN make a hole to the outside, and install a proper vent.

Once, I made a hole through a block wall. I used my hammer drill. I made a big hole by drilling a lot of little holes.

Once I mounted the vent through a basement window. I removed one piece of glass, replaced it with plywood, and cut a hole in the plywood.

## Chute

Is there a laundry chute? Some people just throw things down the steps, and they're always walking on a pile of laundry at the bottom of the steps. Some people keep a big hamper in their bedroom and drag it downstairs.

Look for the possibility of a laundry chute. Is there a bathroom above? It's probable, since builders tend to cluster all the plumbing together. If so, can you cut a hole in the floor? In the bottom of the vanity cabinet? In a linen closet?

## Dryer vent

The dryer vent pipe is clogged with lint. No need to check. They ALL are!

You can buy a cleaning kit. It's a rotating brush and some flexible extension rods that attach to your drill.

You can disconnect the vent at the dryer and hook up your shop vac. Then the brush shakes the lint loose and the shop vac sucks it up.

OR, you can work from the outside, with a draw-string bag. Leave the vent hose hooked up and let the dryer blow the lint to the bag. But in almost every job so far, this method was impractical, because the vent was so close to the ground.

You should clean from the lint filter hole all the way to the great outdoors.

THIS is your free thing! No, wait! Some companies charge $200 for this!

And you will be such a hero, too, since you saved their house from burning down!

### Dryer filter

You should clean the lint filter EVERY LOAD! Pull it out and look. I bet the lint is thicker than a sock. How's the dryer supposed to blow through this? Drying takes a lot longer and costs a lot more.

THIS is your free thing! No, this is too easy. This doesn't count. Do THIS free thing for free!

### Laundry tub

Leaky faucet?

Some older houses have a double basin tub made of cement!

Why not remove it, and replace it with a single-tub vinyl one? Now you have space for another shelving unit. When did they EVER need both tubs?

### Water heater

Is it leaking? Don't wait for a disaster.

Are they running it too hot? You can set these things so high they can scald you. This is extra important if there are very young or very old people there.

### Furnace filter

AH! THIS is your free thing.

Pull out the old filter. It's SURE to be dirty. How dirty? Hold it up to a light. Do they have a spare one on hand? Why not?

Are they aware of the air flow direction? Just remember that "Hot Air Rises". Air flows down the duct, into the furnace, gets heated, and rises UP, UP, and AWAY!

### Humidifier filter

If they have a humidifier, its filter is sure to be clogged with salt.

The average homeowner can change a furnace filter, if they would only get around to it. But most cannot change this one. But YOU can.

### End Of Another Section

Are you on your FOURTH beer already? Did you start with a six pack?

That was a short section, and the next two are short too. Can't you wait a few minutes?

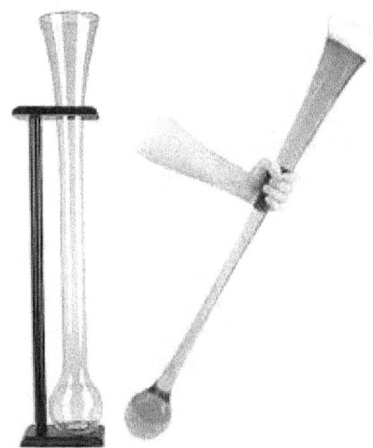

This one is called "A Yard Of Beer". It can hold three cans of beer.

It's actually a practical joke. That bulb at the end holds a bubble of beer. And when it lets go, you're gonna get a face full.

What a waste of three cans of beer! On the other hand, after your first ten beers, nobody will care.

# Stairs

We're talking about the cellar stairs AND the stairs to the second floor. This section has two columns.

**Rail**

IS there a rail? Is it wiggly?

A loose rail is worse than NO rail! At least if there's no rail, people KNOW there's no rail. A bad rail just hangs there on one loose screw, waiting to fool somebody.

**Baby gate**

Is there a baby gate?

TEST IT! Give it a good jerk! Better you than the baby!

**Steps**

Are the steps solid? Or cracked?

I get truly nervous on some basement steps. They look like they're held together with one nail. And I don't trust that nail.

And here's another reminder why you're walking around with the challenge sheet on your clipboard. As you walk around in the bedrooms, you would not notice an attic access that you don't see, would you? If you saw it, you'd point out how bad it was. But out of sight is out of mind.

# Garage

### Shelving

Look for a wasted wall. Some people mount a board on a block wall, and then they can hang rakes and brooms on the board. This is a waste of a perfectly good, long wall.

Suggest one of these:

And then line that wall with shelves, and you can get a TON of stuff up off the floor.

And if there ARE shelves, look if they're being wasted with junk. Ask, "Are you ever going to use this stuff?"

And the garage is another opportunity to point out that missing shed.

How many rusted cans of paint do you see? Why are they keeping them? The paint is sure to be bad. They will have to dispose of it when they sell.

I never did understand the problem with throwing away old paint. If you toss a half a can, you are evil. But if you put that paint onto some old plywood, even if it's twenty coats thick, you are allowed to toss that plywood.

Well, I asked our garbage man why, and here's the answer: They don't want that half-can to be crushed, and to leak out onto the street. They have no problem tossing the paint!

In fact, you can buy a chemical that solidifies paint so you can toss it! Well, air can dry up paint, too! Slather it onto a plywood scrap, and toss the plywood

SO, if you see twenty cans of paint, offer to dispose of them. Not for free. You now know something that the homeowner does not know.

## Opener

Is there an opener? They're not hard to install.

Is it adjusted? When the door is closed, is the chain drooping? That's an indication that it's closing too hard.

 Is there an outside keypad opener? They have remote ones that need no through-the-wall wiring.

If the lady ASSUMES wiring is required on these things, then THAT'S the reason she never installed one. On the other hand, I've been in two houses where the people did not know the code, and did not know how to program it, even though the instructions are right there on the remote.

Can you hit the button to close the door, and get out before the door closes? Sometimes the button is far away from the garage door, and you feel like Indiana Jones, running and ducking under a closing door. And Indiana didn't have to jump over one of those ankle-biting death rays!

It's easy to install a second button near the garage door. Just get a doorbell button, and run two wires to the same two screws as the other button. Now you can step out into the driveway, reach in, and close the door.

## Springs

Pull the opener's red rope, so you can open the door manually.

Lift the door. CAN you lift the door? A seven-year old girl should be able to lift it.

Lift the door half way, and let it go. It should stay there, and not drop back down. If it's too heavy, the opener is being strained. The opener isn't supposed to lift a great weight. It's only supposed to move a balanced door back and forth.

You can adjust the springs. Open the door so the springs are relaxed. If there is no opener, lock the door in position with a C-clamp or a vice-grips on the track. Unhook the cable using the S hook at the house end (not at the bottom of the door), and shorten the cable. Make both springs the same length, and therefore the same strength, so the door doesn't go up crooked.

## Safety cables

These are cables that run THROUGH each spring. In normal operation, the spring just slides along this cable, and the cable has no apparent function.

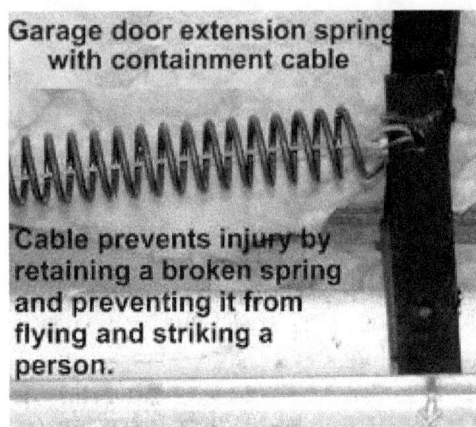
Garage door extension spring with containment cable

Cable prevents injury by retaining a broken spring and preventing it from flying and striking a person.

Until a spring breaks! Then it supports the spring so it doesn't drop down and swing like tarzan.

This actually happened to me once! It didn't hit me, but I felt the wind, and it did scare the hell out of me.

Think about it... When would a rusty old hinge break? Not in the middle of the night. It would be when it gets stretched out that one last time. That's when someone closes the garage door. It's not unlikely that a person would be standing there when the garage door closes.

SO! You are careful to say, "Lady, we must tighten your springs, because you are wearing out your opener. But I cannot tighten them unless we install safety cables, for my own safety."

### Car inside

Can they get the car inside? Both cars?

If not, they REALLY need a shed! Garages are for cars. Sheds are for all this crap that keeps the car outside.

### *NOW* It's Time To Take A Break!

Three small sections were as much work a one big one. You've earned your fifth beer.

I'm not sure about this chess set. If I take your piece, do I get to drink that beer? Or do I make YOU drink that beer?

And the king and queen look like mixed drinks. So when you lose, you have to chug the king and queen? After maybe fourteen beers?

Who are we kidding? When the game is over, will we pour the remaining beers down the sink? No, we'll end up drinking it ALL!

You might as well finish this book now. You're not going up any ladders today.

# *Bedrooms*

This section has FOUR columns. But there's room for a fifth, and even more. Some houses are so big they look more like small hotels. But let's not insult the person with only three bedrooms.

It's important to do each and every one of these checks in EVERY bedroom.

## Doors and Door knobs

We already handled these above, in the main living area.

Except for one thing: Is there a robe hook on the door? I like bars that have several hooks.

Do they open smoothly? Are they dragging on carpet? Do they close? Do they lock?

Is there some smashed drywall where the doorknob hits? The best doorstop attaches to the wall at exactly that spot. Another EASY job. It might even cover up the drywall damage.

## Closet doors

Bi-fold door are always out of whack. There are always adjustments.

Start with the hinge side. The top bracket should not be loose, so it can slide along the upper track.

There might be a track on the bottom, or you could be looking at a cheaper door with a bottom pivot:

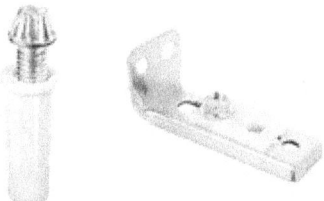

The bottom pivot is also a height adjustment. On better doors there's a screwdriver adjustment.

You want the hinge side to be vertical, higher than the carpet, and as close to the wall as you can get, still allowing clearance.

You can make these adjustments while the sliding side is out of the track, so the door is hanging out into the room.

Now the other side of the door should ride in the track at a constant height. If it gets lower or higher as the door closes, you are not vertical on the hinge side.

## Organizer

If there's clutter on the floor, they need an organizer.

If it's a kid's room, how do they expect the kid to keep the room clean if there isn't a place for everything?

### Mini blinds and Drape rods

Do they work? Do mini blinds have missing slats? Do the pull strings still work on the drape rods?

### Paddle fan

Is it going the right direction? We talked about this before. If the little switch is up, then air is blowing up. Most people want a fan when they are hot and want to cool off.

IS there a fan? One over the bed is perfect. There's nothing better than lying under a big fan on a warm night. It's better than air conditioning.

See part 3.

### Wall paper

Like I said above, I like to remove wallpaper, but I hate to install it.

Is it peeling? Torn? Are THEY sick of it?

### Patch & Paint

Covered above. But look at the walls and point out some damage.

### Carpet

I don't do carpet. There's too much to know, and too many special tools for a once-in-a-while "specialty".

### Another Break Already?

Yes, this was a short section. But you DID have to inspect TEN things in each of FOUR bedrooms.

So Yes! Time for the fifth beer!

And the end is in sight!

 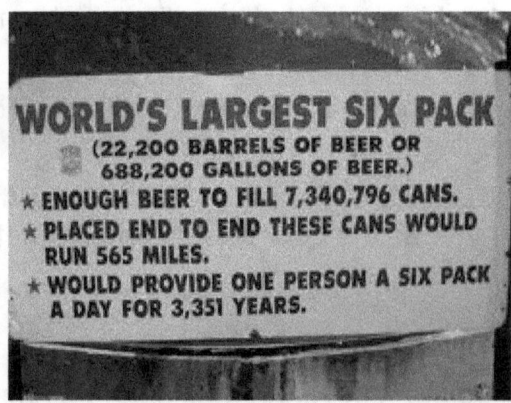

68

# *Baths*

Check all baths, even the powder room downstairs, and the powder room in the basement.

## Medicine chest

Some people make do with a mirror. Make them imagine how nice it would be to have some shelves behind that mirror.

Some people make do with an old rusty medicine chest. One of those "nobody will ever see this thing" things.

This is another job I would never do without my third hand. See the tip in Part 4.

This reminds me of an excellent practical joke. A woman suspected her friend was snooping in her medicine chest. Nosy. Looking at prescriptions, feminine products, whatever.

She removed the shelves, drilled a hole in the top, made sure the magnetic catch was adjusted strong, and poured in some marbles!

When the guy opened the door, the marbles fell out! BUSTED!

Pretty good? Almost as good as saran wrap over the toilet bowel.

Almost as good as taping the trigger open on a kitchen sink sprayer.

But I digress.

## Paddle Fan

Why not in the bathroom? It's a great place to stand when you are moist.

## Faucet & Vanity

I've learned a few plumbing tips. See Part 4.

## Toilet

Is it running? It could be three things:

Maybe the flapper valve is leaking. Does the toilet run once in a while, then shut off again? That's cycling. Then you have a slow leak.

Does it run and run, once in a while, but normally it's OK? Then maybe the flapper chain is too long, and sometimes it gets under the flapper.

Or maybe the shut-off valve is set to the wrong depth. I've seen them set so high that the water level is higher than the overflow tube. This tank will NEVER get full. The water will never get high enough to shut off the valve. Just adjust the level.

Or maybe the valve is too old. If you raise the float and it doesn't shut off, you need a new valve.

Does the toilet flush inadequately? Do you have to flush twice for a number two? If the lady is getting on in years, a taller toilet is better.

You can replace a toilet. It's not hard. But it's possible to do it wrong. If that wax ring doesn't seat properly, you'll never know it until you have a leak.

Once you replace a few, it becomes easy. But how do you get through those first few? Take a chance, or pass.

By the way, if an older woman would like a taller toilet, here's an easier solution:

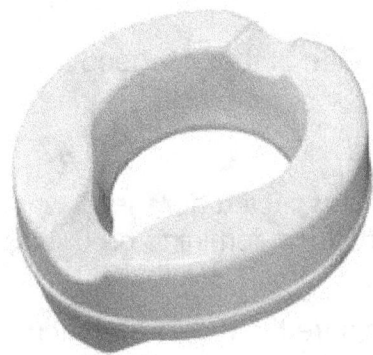

Guests can lift it off. She can bring this along when she travels or visits.

### Toilet seat

There's a new kind of seat out there! And you thought they had perfected the toilet seat, didn't you?

They come with two buttons. You install these two buttons on the toilet bowl. They fit tight and don't slip around.

Then you attach the seat to the buttons. It's easy to detach the seat from the buttons, clean underneath, and replace it, without tools.

### Shower head

Do they have a showerhead? Suggest a hand-held one! It's easy and fun to hit those hard-to-reach places.

Ask if they get enough water? Does it take ten minutes to rinse their hair? I like to remove that water-saving gizmo. Yes, they save water, but water is not scarce where I live. And running a water saving shower for an extra ten minutes doesn't save any water, does it?

### Wall paper

One last time... I hate wallpaper. It seems to be its worst in bathrooms, probably from the humidity.

Suggest that paint might be better.

### Door

Does this door close and lock? It's pretty important that this door locks. Even if your family is "friendly," your guests won't understand.

### Closet door

Is there a linen closet? Does this door work? Is there a robe hook or two? Is this an opportunity for a laundry chute?

### Caulk

Caulking a tub is easy. You can use your finger to shmoosh it, or you can be a professional and use a tool:

Five bucks. Includes a caulk remover, too.

### GFI

Is there an outlet?

Is it a GFI? If it is not a GFI, test it. If your tester shows there's a good ground, it is easy to swap out the old and swap in the new.

What? There's no outlet? How do you curl your hair? Or straighten your hair? Whichever the case may be. And either way, how do you DRY your hair?

We have four outlets in our bathroom (2 duplex outlets), and it's not enough. How do people live with ZERO outlets?

Some old light fixtures and medicine chests have an outlet. These are VERY old. You can't buy these anymore. And that's probably why the lady can't toss that rusty medicine chest. She would be tossing her only outlet.

Sometimes it's possible to add an outlet.  A GFI outlet, of course.

There's a light switch, right? It might be hot. You have to open it up and look.

If the power comes in at the switch, and they ran a cable up to the light, you're in business.

You need one of these:

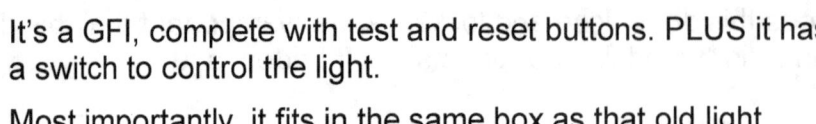

It's a GFI, complete with test and reset buttons. PLUS it has a switch to control the light.

Most importantly, it fits in the same box as that old light switch!

I could NEVER go from four outlets to one. But the person who has NONE would JUMP at the chance to move up to one!

On the other hand, it's possible that the power comes in at the light, and then they ran a wire down to the switch. If that's the case, you can't use one of these, but you are NOT dead:

You can remove the medicine chest! You will see a big gaping hole.

You can reach up and have easy access to the light above. You can drill a hole in the stud, giving you easy access to the wall beside the medicine chest.

Now you can install a new box on the side, and wire it up at the light fixture

And as a bonus, you can replace that old medicine chest, too! Get one that's bigger, and is surface mount, covering that big gaping hole. If it has three mirrors, you can even see the back of your head!

**Grab Bars**

Grab bars are easy to install. But the old lady has no idea, so she lives without them.

Did you ever see a toilet paper holder that's been ripped out of the wall? How did that happen? Looks like someone needed a grab bar.

Just be sure to drill right into a solid stud. No plastic plugs allowed here.

Maybe you could put one in a place that makes it easier to get on and off the toilet AND in and out of the tub.

Maybe you could install TWO grab bars. Or even THREE!

## *Finished!*

Congrats!

Now how many of those jobs have you done around your own house? You knew you were handy, but I bet you never made a list before.

And how many of those jobs need to be done around your house? The shoemaker's kids...

What WILL you do with all those empty beer cans???

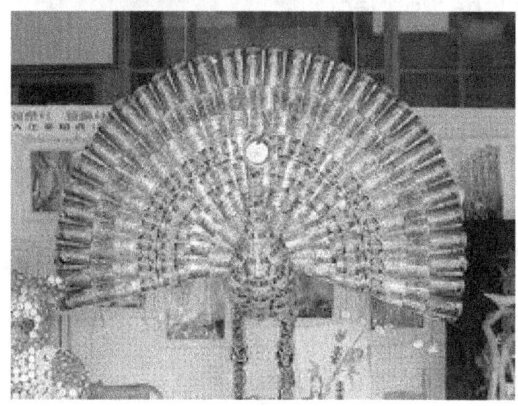

# PART THREE

# Jack Of All Trades,
# And Master Of One

So now you can place an ad for a handyman, and you will get some calls, and you will be able to do that job.

But it's also nice to have a specialty. Or two.

Take my favorite job, furniture assembly:

1.  I can place an ad that talks only about furniture assembly. It is not somewhere in a list of 100 jobs I can do.

2.  I can add pictures to my ad. Pictures of finished projects.

3.  I get calls for the job I like. People call on the catch-all ad give me jobs, but more calls come in for my favorite job.

4.  The more assemblies I do, the better I get.

5.  I learn tricks. I buy tools. I am better at this than anybody.

6.  There is little competition. Go to your local craigs list and search for furniture assembly. I rarely see ads for other assemblers. I see a lot of ads for stores SELLING furniture that must be assembled.

7.  I like installing TV wall mounts. I stock a couple of each kind. I can provide a mount, at a profit, if the customer doesn't want to shop for one. Now, the best prices are at Amazon. I cannot buy a mount when a call comes in and wait a week for delivery. I cannot stock everything for every job (mail box posts, attic steps, etc.), but I can stock what I need for one or two specialties.

8.  When you've done a dozen TV wall mounts (or assembled a dozen swing sets, etc.) you know how long it takes. You don't have to rely on the hourly charge thing because you don't know how long something takes. I use the hourly on most jobs, but I have fixed prices for my specialty jobs.

**I have THREE specialties.**

Jobs I like to do. Jobs I've gotten good with.

1.  Furniture Assembly,

2.  TV Wall Mounts

3.  Ceiling Fans.

And I'm still deciding about attic steps and wallpaper removal.

They both qualify. They are jobs most people won't do, but if you do a few, they become easy.

# *Furniture Assembly*

### Tip 1 – My best tip

One day I had to assemble a microwave cart and a hutch.

I started with the cart.

I spread out all the parts, laid out my tools, sat down on the floor, and got busy. It wasn't long before I had to get up to get a tool. Then get up to get the next part. And so on.

Finally finished, it was time to start on the hutch. And it hit me! I used the cart as a worktable. I didn't have to sit on the floor! More importantly, I didn't have to get up and down. A part or a tool was only a step away. It wasn't the best table, since it was so small. But it was better than nothing.

I have used beds to assemble furniture in a bedroom. (BTW – if you DO use a bed as a worktable, don't put your tools on the bedspread. Even if you took the trouble to BOIL your tools the night before, if the woman comes in and sees you, she'll have a conniption.)

I have even used an ironing board as a worktable.

Then I had a BRILLIANT idea! I started to carry two card tables! Now I carry a folding six-foot work table AND a card table (for parts and tools).

This is one of those moments, like the invention of the wheel. Once you see it, it's obvious. But until you see it, you never think to bring your own tables.

It's obvious to use any table that's nearby. But to bring a table to use when there is no table nearby is a good idea.

I used my two card tables to assemble a sandbox. Now THAT'S not obvious! Wouldn't you spread everything out on the driveway and get started?

This guy is NOT using my best tip.

This guy did not read this book!

**Tip 2 – Picture Orientation.**

You should lay the parts out in the right direction so they LOOK like the picture.

Let's say you're looking at a side wall of a book shelf.

The picture has two cam lock studs on the bottom, which is on the left, then there is a dowel almost in the middle on the far edge, etc.

But that part is pointing the other way on your worktable. No problem. If those cam locks go on the left end in the picture, then they'd be on the right end, right?

And so on.

What a waste of brainpower. What an opportunity to screw up.

Just turn the piece around, so it looks like the picture. The work goes faster, and with no errors. Remember, a mistake often requires undoing several steps.

**Tip 3 – Electric screwdriver.**

It's never in the list of required tools, but I consider it a required tool.

One day it occurred to me that whenever I'm assembling furniture, I'm always indoors, and there's always an outlet nearby. WHY am I constantly recharging my electric screwdriver?

You CAN use your electric drill, but your drill is too powerful. You can screw in a cam lock post so fast and powerfully that you actually blow out the hole.

It is OK to use a drill that has a clutch. Adjust it to a light setting, so once the cam lock is screwed in, the drill quits trying so hard.

**Tip 4 – Allen wrenches.**

Some furniture comes with an allen wrench or two. I toss them. Or give them to the lady, for her shoebox collection of tools. But I never use them.

I have a set of allen wrenches that fit my drill! I have a set of star drive bits, too. And two square drive bits. And socket drivers.

## TV Wall Mounts

**Work Table**

First, I use a work table. The one that's always in my van. See "furniture assembly", above.

AND I bring a blanket. They don't want their screen scratched when I place the TV face down on the table. Now, the screen will NOT get scratched. There is a lip all the way around the TV; the glass does not touch the table. Still, it looks like I care when I spread out my blanket.

I put the table near the wall, pointing towards the wall, but not touching the wall. I want to be able to walk between the table and the wall.

Place the TV on the table, with the bottom edge along the wall. So you will be ready to tip the TV up vertically, and then lift it onto the bracket.

## The TV Half Of The Bracket

The bracket comes with a dozen screws. Pick the ones that fit the four holes on the TV. And answer me this question: Why doesn't the TV manufacturer provide those four screws? They know what size they need! Why does the bracket manufacturer have to provide a dozen different sizes??? In fact, why don't they use the same four screws that hold the foot onto the TV? No, that would be too logical.

If there are short screws and long screws that fit those holes, choose the long screws, and use the spaces if necessary. If the TV is too close to the wall, it could be hard to attach the wires and cables.

Which way should the bracket point? Think about how it will hook onto the bracket.

Which is left and right? If there are knobs to tighten the tilt mechanism, make sure these knobs are on the outside.

## Do The Math

I used to draw pictures and do quite a bit of math. Then I found a short cut.

Place the wall half of the bracket onto the TV, as it will be when the job is done.

Measure the height of the TV. Hold your tape measure with the end at the top of the TV and your thumb marking the bottom of the TV. This doesn't have to be perfect.

Now look at where the top screw holes are on the bracket. Let's say the holes are at 12 inches, and the TV is 30 inches tall.

Now go to the wall and hold the tape where the TV will be. Tell them that this tape represents the TV is it high enough? A little higher? A little lower? If it's over a fireplace mantle, remind them that they might want something on the mantle, which should not block their view of the screen.

When they say you've found the right place, make a pencil mark at the 12 inch mark. THAT'S where you will drill your holes.

## Find The Studs

Just be sure you find a stud. PS – make sure you find the WHOLE stud. You MUST go into the MIDDLE of the stud. It's possible that you go in, but you go in too close to the edge. It feels right while you're screwing it in, but it ain't right.

For drywall, the best way is to find the stud with a stud finder. Then use an ice pick.

Dig it in through the drywall, as if you were gouging out somebody's eyeball. You will find solid wood, or you will find dead air. Move left and right, gouging several holes. You will find the stud, and you will find dead air at each side of the stud. When you are done, you will have five or six holes. You will know EXACTLY where that stud is. And the wall mount will hide those extra holes.

Plaster is too hard to poke with an ice pick, and most stud finders don't work very well. The plaster is too thick, and not a constant density like drywall. You have to drill a line of pilot holes. But like with the ice pick, you will find air, then you will find solid wood. You still have to find both sides of the stud.

One clue to a starting point is an outlet. Imagine this wall before the plaster. You can see the studs. And an outlet is nailed to a stud. You just don't know if the stud is to the right or left of the outlet. Another clue is a furnace register.

One warning for plaster walls: don't be fooled by the lath sticks.

Before drywall, this is how they applied plaster. First, they nail lath sticks to the studs. Then they smoosh the plaster between the sticks. This picture is from behind the wall. Now, when you drill, looking for wood, you will think you have found wood, when actually you only found a lath stick. This is not enough meat to do the job. You HAVE to find a stud. As you drill, you will feel some wood, and then and then you will feel dead air.

For the second stud, know that most walls are 16 inches "on center". It's 16 inches from the center of one stud to the center of the next. Or, it's 16 inches from the left side of one stud to the left side of the next. It's NOT 16 inches BETWEEN the studs.

For brick walls (and that includes brick walls that are covered with a coating of plaster), you can go wherever you want. You need a hammer drill, and a masonry bit. You will be using plastic plugs or lead shields and lag bolts.

For brick walls, do NOT use an articulated mount. Imagine a heavy TV with the arm stretched out. That's quite a bit of leverage, pulling that wall mount out of the wall.

## Placing the bracket

I used to drill the first hole, screw in the first lag bolt, hold a level on the bracket, level the bracket, and drill the second hole.

The problem is that the drill might have walked a littler. And now the bracket is not exactly level any more.

It's a small error, when you're looking at the bracket, but when you hang a 70" TV, the error is magnified.

I came up with a brilliantly simple idea: I hold the bracket on the wall, and I hammer in a finishing nail through the slot. Just don't go where you plan to drill. Now level the bracket and drive in a second nail. Now the bracket is level.

Drill the top two holes, and screw in the two lags, but don't tighten them yet. Look at those two nails. Is the bracket resting on both nails?

If not, then your drill walked a little. And you can't redrill one of those holes to move it a little. You will just end up with a bigger hole.

But you do have a second chance. You can drill one of the lower two holes to correct the error. The slots are a little bigger than the lags. If the right side is too low, drill the lower right hole a little higher. It does not matter if the bracket is resting on the top two lags. It is resting on two lags, and four lags will be holding it tight against the wall.

If you screw up again, you can start all over, an inch higher or lower than your first attempt. Isn't it nice that the lady isn't watching you work?

When you are done, you should have FOUR lag bolts, all solidly in studs, and the bracket is level. Some brackets allow a little adjustment, but most do not.

## Hang The TV

Usually, the homeowner will help. Just explain how even if you could lift this thing, you'd never be able to see behind it. And they are always present. They NEVER leave you alone; they want to be sure it is mounted exactly where they want it. And they want to be there to hook up their cables the way they want.

Drag the table closer to the wall, stand the TV up, and you only have to lift it from the table to the bracket.

So I lift one side, and the homeowner lifts the other. I let the homeowner hang their hook on their side first. I can see what they're doing, and I can direct them. And the first one is the easy one. Let them do the easy one.

## A One-Man Show

It CAN be done with one person. I would never do this with someone watching, because it looks scary. But if someone is watching, they can help, and I wouldn't HAVE to do this.

I use ropes and S hooks.

Drag the table to the wall, and stand it up. It is leaning on the wall. Let's start on the right side. I place an S hook on the bracket, and another on the bracket hook on the TV. Tie a rope to the wall's S hook. Loop it under the TV's S hook. Lift the TV up two feet, and tie a knot.

Now the left side of the TV is resting on the table, the right side is two feet higher, and you can let go. The TV isn't going anywhere.

Now walk around the table to the other side. You may be able to lift the left side up to the bracket. The right side is two feet high. You should be able to lift the left side all the way up to the bracket. If not, use two more S hooks, another rope, and take an extra step.

And go read that section about insurance again.

### Finishing Touches

Some brackets have screws you tighten so the TV stays put.

Some have tilt. Tilt the TV so there is no glare from a window, and tighten the lock knobs.

If the TV is a little crooked, in spite of all your efforts, and there is no adjustment, I have slipped a finishing nail UNDER the hook on the low side.

Some TV's look crooked, yet your level says they are correct. It turns out the HOUSE is a little crooked! The ceiling is not exactly level. Ask the lady, do you want it to be right? Or do you want it to LOOK right?

You should fill your extra drill holes. I carry a caulking gun.

And you should clean up your dust. Sometimes the homeowner is happy to do it, but I carry a dust buster.

### Wire Hiding

This is an upsell some people want. You should have one hider on hand.

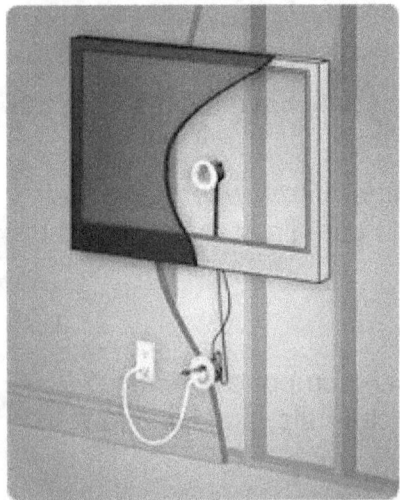

I've tried a few, and this one is the best. The brand name is Legrand.

They give you a hole saw, which you might already have from a doorknob job. They give you a handle for the hole saw. But I leave this at home, and use my drill. I don't want the job to look TOO easy.

The top piece has a place to plug in the TV, and a hole to drop your low voltage wires through.

Then you drop some electrical cable(provided) down to the lower piece, and wire it up. The bottom piece has a place to plug in that extension cord. The extension cord has to reach an outlet. We do not play with the household wiring. We don't even turn off a breaker.

The homeowner places a small table under the TV to hold the cable box etc. Then you don't see the lower unit.

### Surface Hiding

This kind is easier, and may be the only way possible. It's so easy, that the homeowner can do it. I've only done this once for one customer who didn't want to bother.

You can paint it, if you want.

They have kits with angles. You can go down to the floor, follow the baseboard, etc.

# *Ceiling Fans*

### Don't Use An Old Ceiling Light's Box?

If there is a ceiling light, it's easy to install a fan. You can attach it to the existing electrical box.

They warn you not to do it. After all, the light weighs one pound. The fan weighs ten pounds, and it's a moving object.

You're supposed to buy a bracket, remove the existing box, and hang the fan from the bracket.

There is no need to go up into the attic. You can remove the old box, and put it up through the hole. Use a wrench on that square bar to spread it out between two joists. The teeth on the ends bite into the joist.

### But I Do It All The Time

I have such a bracket. I bought it years ago. I'm still waiting for a chance to use it.

Remove an old box, and you will understand. The old guy who installed the old box used two nails into a joist. You would need a crow bar to remove it.

And you would use the crow bar to pull the box horizontally, AWAY from the joist, pulling the nails OUT of the joist.

You cannot remove the box by pulling it straight down. And that's exactly what the fan would be trying to do.

And they always warn you that the fan is a moving object. So what? It runs silently. It doesn't vibrate.

They might have a point If the box is NOT nailed to a joist. If it's attached to the ceiling, the nails would be pointing UP. But there is no wood above the box! They always nailed the box to the joist.

### Buy Some Screws

Every fan says you are to attach the fan to the electrical box using the two screws that come with the box.

You often find that those two screws are missing.

Buy a few screws. You need 8-32. Buy several different lengths. Sometimes there ARE screws, but they're too short.

### If There Is No Ceiling Light

I would use that bracket if there were no light.

The good news is you can make a hole wherever you want.

The bad news is that you need to get power to it. You have to get up into the attic. See the next section.

# *Attic*

I'm still deciding if attic steps should be another specialty. If the other three don't pull enough gigs, I'll start. All it takes is one more ad on craigslist.

How do you get into the attic? Some attics have a trap door in a closet. The builder hid it so it wouldn't be an eyesore. But you can't use it! How do you wiggle a big box up over that closet shelf and into that tiny hole? Don't you have to empty the closet shelf first?

You don't have to go as far as a folding ladder. You get the same access with a big trap door and a stepladder.

You don't have to tamper with the joists. Just cut through the drywall. Line the hole with 1x4's, to make a lip for the lid to rest on.

Then trim the edges. It doesn't have to be a picture frame like this. It can be more 1x4's, with butt joints.

Folding stairs ARE the best. It's a bigger job and a bigger ticket.

I don't like to cut the joists. You can watch a lot of Youtubes, and they do it all the time. But don't most houses have trusses? Those big triangles? And aren't you cutting one or two of those triangles? And could a huge snow load cause some damage? Still, everybody does it.

But I won't.

They make ladders that fit between the joists. You just have to find a spot where the joists run the right way. The homeowner might want to use the hallway, but I won't do it if I have to cut two joists. Ladders can also go in the extra bedroom.

## The One-Man Show

Watch a few Youtubes, and they all require two people; one up in the attic and one down below. You cut the hole, lift the ladder up into the attic, and the upstairs guy attaches the header. Then you can open the ladder, and the upstairs guy can come down. You need the downstairs guy to remove the temporary supports so the ladder can open.

But the job CAN be done with one guy! I use two support sticks like everybody else, but I place mine so the ladder can open. There is plenty of wood on both sides to support the ladder, and still leave room at both ends for the ladder to open.

Another trick is to prestart 3 screws into the header.

SO...

1.  Measure the opening exactly, so the ladder will be able to open. Place your two support sticks.

2.  Lift the ladder up into the attic, and then lower it onto your support sticks. Push it all the way to the header. The rear support stick is still holding up the other end.

3.  Now open the first section of the ladder.

4.  Put your stepladder as close as possible to the half-open ladder, and you can reach those 3 screws with a long screw driver bit. Push the ladder up against the header, centered, and drive in those three screws.

The other end of the ladder frame doesn't support anything. But it must be square so the ladder's cover door fits. So close the ladder now, and that far end will square itself. Push in some shims, open the ladder, and attach those shims.

### The Feet

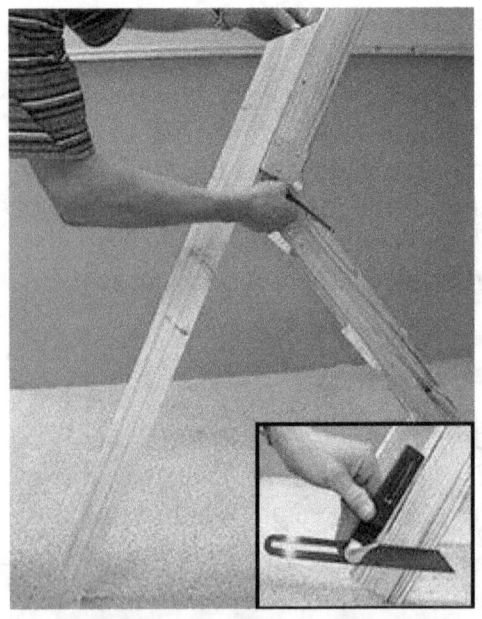

I failed once with an aluminum ladder. They are nice, because the feet attachments are at the perfect angle. And you can have any height you want; just slide them up or down and drill them in.

The problem was that I had to remove the bottom step. It was in the way of this cute idea. And now it was too high to step to the first step.

I only do wooden ones now. I can cut anywhere I want. I would only have to remove the last step if it were ON the carpet.

How to measure:

For the length, fold up the bottom section, and use a trim piece as a straightedge and measure down to the floor. Cutting wood is easy. It's easy to leave it a half inch too long, open the ladder completely, stand on it, and see how it works. The hinge between the top and middle sections, and the hinge between the middle and bottom sections should both be closed. If there's a gap, you are not done.

For the angle, use an angle copier.

23053

You can always carry some plastic feet, for when you screw up.

OR, you can PLAN on using these when the ladder is landing on a hardwood floor.

# *Wallpaper Removal*

I'm still deciding if wallpaper removal should be another specialty.

Some kinds of paper peel off in big sections. Some kinds come off in postage stamp sizes. People never seem to call me to remove the easy kind. They usually try to remove the hard kind, but then give up when they see how hard it is.

I LOVE to remove wallpaper, but I HATE applying new wallpaper. It seems easy, but then the edges curl. So I tell people that. "It's my mission in life to eradicate all wallpaper." Then they can call somebody ELSE to apply the new paper. Or let me paint. Or the homeowner wants to paint; they just couldn't remove the paper.

### Remove The First Layer

Those tiger paw things don't work. They make lots of holes, but you can't get enough of the solution in behind the paper.

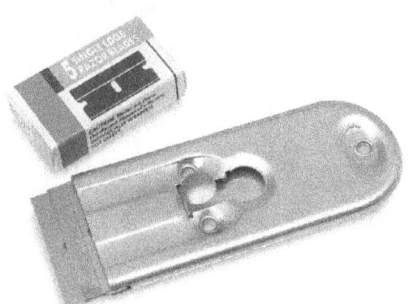

You have to take this kind off with a razor blade.

Here's the best way to scrape wallpaper:

I hold it at a 45 degree angle, and push upwards, like a snow plow.

Walk along with a trash can.

### Remove The Second Layer

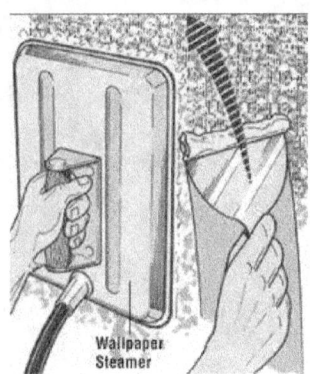

Wallpaper Steamer

But then you're left with that brown paper.

Get a steamer. Your customer will NOT buy a steamer. They won't even think of it. Even if they do, they don't want to buy a machine that they will only use once. Silly people… You charge more for one hour than this thing costs!

You hold it against the paper for a few seconds. Then you move it to the next section while you're removing the moist paper from the last section with your putty knife.

Walk along with a trash can.

### Finish

You still have to wash the wall with some DIF solution to remove the last of the glue.

And you might have to patch a few gouges. Some gouges were made by the homeowner, when THEY were trying to remove the paper.

# PART FOUR

# Tips, Tricks, And Cool Tools

I know how to paint, patch drywall, and do basic plumbing. But I don't like these jobs. So I wouldn't call these my specialties.

Still, I have learned a few tips, which I'll pass along here.

I have come across some cool tools, too.

## *How To Patch A Drywall Hole*

Nail holes can be filled with mud. Doorknob bashes can be covered with tape and mud, or better yet, a door stop. But some holes need a new piece of drywall.

You can cut a plug piece about the size of the hole. But how do you support it from behind?

The best way I found was to put a paint-stirring stick in the hole behind the wall, and hold it in place with two drywall screws. So you have two screws on the good part of the wall, holding a stick at the perfect depth. Put in your plug, one more drywall screw to hold it in place, then tape, mud, and you are done.

**I HATE Drywall Repair.**

You have to apply the mud, and wait for it to dry. Then sand it, apply a thinner coat, and wait again. You might be done, or you might need a third shot. But don't you see? You don't want to make three trips to this place. It wasn't a problem when you were working on your own house.

My friend swears by the quick set stuff. But it comes in a powder, you have to mix it, and it's harder to work.

I like to tell people that I will repair their wall if I could do several other jobs, too. Do the original repair and apply the first coat of mud. Then set up a 20-inch box fan to blow at it. While it dries, install a ceiling fan. Now come back and do the second coat, and fix a sticking door while the second coat dries. Get it? Maybe you have to come back once, but not thrice.

Otherwise I DECLINE! Thanks but no thanks. I tell people I'm not good at it, and they thank me for my honesty, and for not inflicting a bad job on them.

AND, I have patched the big hole, applied the first coat of mud, and left them with some sandpaper and a zip-lock bag of mud. They don't mind. They just didn't know how to patch the big hole. They understand that I don't want to make three trips, and they don't want to PAY for three trips.

# *Painting Tips*

Everybody can paint. Except the old lady, or the busy exec. etc.

## Tape

If you're going to use masking tape, apply it all before you start to paint. Then remove it as soon as you apply paint. Don't let it dry, or the paint will grow a raised edge.

There is a tape for baseboards. It's about 3 inches wide and the adhesive is only on  one edge, for about a half-inch. You stick it on the top of the baseboards. It makes a little shelf that catches drips. But again, you paint and you remove immediately.

Here's a trick that I have not tried, but it sounds good. Let's say the wall will be blue and the ceiling will be white. Start with the ceiling. Paint some white onto the wall, which will be covered soon. Now apply your tape to the ceiling, so when you paint the wall, and remove the tape, you should not see any blue paint on the ceiling. The problem is that you DO see some blue on the ceiling! It leaked under that tape, which is not an air-tight seal. The trick is to paint the tape and the wall with some more white paint. White paint will leak trough just like the blue did. But white is no problem. After the white paint dries, paint blue onto the wall and onto the tape.

## Tapeless

You don't need masking tape. You need the brush with its bristles cut on a diagonal. You can cut in so close you won't need tape anymore. Don't start a line with a fully loaded brush. And hold it perpendicular to the wall you're painting. For example, if you're cutting in near door trim, the brush should be perpendicular to the wall, not at a 45 degree angle into that wall / trim joint.

If the walls and ceilings are different colors, it is impossible to make a perfect line. Should you err with a little wall paint on the ceiling? Or with a little ceiling paint on the wall? Imagine standing across the room, looking at the wall from a distance. If you have a little ceiling paint on the wall, people will see it from a distance, because they're looking right at the wall. But if you have a little wall paint on the ceiling, it's too oblique to see from a distance. Now if the person walks right up to the wall, and looks up, you can't win. But nobody does.

## Extension Sticks

Use an extension stick in your roller handle, even if you can reach where you're painting. Some people use one only for ceilings. I use mine all the time. I get better leverage, and I don't have to bend over to dip, or to reach the bottom section of the wall.

I have a short stick for confined spaces, like in a hallway. I will hold the roller handle only when there is no other way.

I bought a stick. Broomsticks and mop handles work for a while, but the wood is so soft they don't last very long. I wonder if it's real wood. The stick I bought has a metal end.

## Rolling

Everybody tells you to define a section, maybe 3 feet wide and half of the wall high.
1. Make a big "W" in the upper section,
2. Then go across, spreading the paint uniformly,
3. Then go up and down, removing the roller marks.
4. Then repeat on the lower section.

That's good. But this is better:
1. Make your big "W" on the upper section,
2. Go across,
3. Dip again, make another "W" for the lower section,
4. Go across,
5. Finally go up and down in long strokes over both sections, from the floor to the ceiling.

## Ceilings

For white ceilings, there is a paint that goes on pink, and dries white. It is VERY hard to miss a spot.

## Lighting

I have 2 work lights.

Don't try to paint with a table lamp and whatever daylight you have.

If your paint job looks OK under this harsh light, it will be perfect under normal light.

# *How To Install A Mailbox Post*

Those big mailboxes need a 4x4 post sunk into the ground. Then you slip the mailbox over the post, and fasten it with a lag bolt or two.

But how do you sink that 4x4?

- First you have to go get one. They come in 8-foot lengths.

- So you have to cut one. Where do you toss the rest of it? Or do you keep it for your next mailbox job? Are you going into the mailbox business?

- Then you have to dig a hole. Do you have a posthole digger?

- Then you have to mix some concrete. I hope your wheelbarrow doesn't spill. Oh yeah, don't forget your wheelbarrow, a hose, a hoe, and a shovel.

- And where will you dump the excess? And hose off your tools?

- And you have to come back the next day, after the concrete sets.

**OR...**

Buy a post kit! It has about 2 feet of 4x4 at the top, and a metal spike thing on the bottom. Bring your sledgehammer. Pound it in a few inches, check with your level, pound it in some more, and so on. In 5 minutes you'll have a 4x4 post sticking out of the ground.

# How To Repair A Screen

It's EASY!

You need some screen fabric. I like the cloth stuff, rather than the metal stuff.

But if you're repairing some dog damage on a patio sliding door, get the metal stuff.

You can usually use the old cord, which is good, because this stuff comes in several thicknesses.

And you need this tool:

One wheel is concave, and one is convex (one has a groove, one has a round edge).

You need a FLAT surface! Use the porch or driveway.

You DON'T push the cord and the screen into the groove!

First, you push the screen into the groove with the convex end of the tool.

Then you push the cord into that fabric-lined groove with the concave end.

Start on one long edge. Leave an inch or so excess.

Start in the MIDDLE of that long edge, then work outwards.

Then go to the opposite long edge. But DON'T push the fabric into the groove from one end to the other. The fabric will twist the screen out of square. You should push it in at the halfway point, keeping it tight, then at the bottom, then at the top, and then at the quarters. Once you get it seated in there without any twisting, THEN you can think of that wheel as a wheel.

Cutting the excess is the last step.

# *Electrical Testers*

You need these!

### Outlet tester

Just plug it in and look at the lights. It detects the common mistakes that most people make, like reversing white and black, open ground, etc.

We used it above in the challenge to show the lady that her 2-prong adapter was installed incorrectly and was doing no good.

I use it every time I replace an outlet.

### Non-Contact

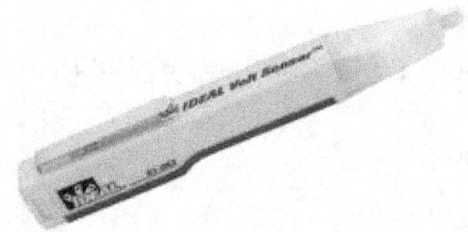

You don't have to strip a wire so you can touch copper. This thing SMELLS electricity, right through the insulation! Actually, it uses induction.

And it beeps and lights up, too!

In some old houses, you can remove a switch, and see only two black wires, not one black and one white. Separate them so there's some distance between them. Hold this tester near each wire, and you will know which one will kill.

I have no idea how this works since the circuit is not complete. You have a wire sticking out into the room. Dead end! But it works.

## Multimeter

Two easy uses:

I test a whole box of used batteries. Set it on DC, 2 volts. Line up the batteries. It doesn't matter which way they point. If you hold the wrong lead on the wrong contact, you just get a negative number.

It's good for continuity testing. Set it on ohms. Touch the two leads together. The reading will jump. (some testers beep). Now touch the two contacts to a switch or something you wonder is continuous. Or not.

## Breaker Finder

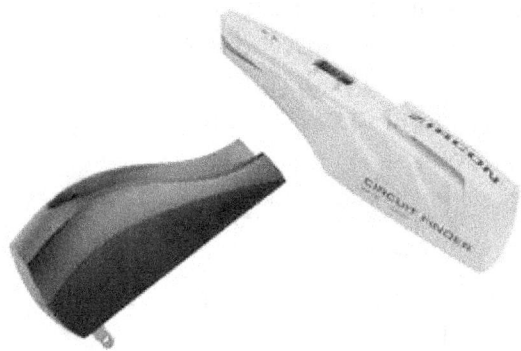

This one is GENIUS! If you want to work on an outlet, you should turn off the breaker. But which one? As you go down the row of breakers, you're turning off computers, VCR's and everything.

OR, you plug the black part into the outlet. If you want to work on a ceiling light fixture, you can unscrew the light bulb, and screw in an adapter that allows you to plug something in.

Now go downstairs. Hold the yellow part against the breakers, and slowly go down the row. When you find the right one, it beeps.

The black thing sends a signal. The yellow thing senses that signal.

It doesn't work on every breaker box, but when it does, you win!

# Third Hand

I first saw one of these at a garage sale. It was stretched across the garage door opening, and they had clothes hung on it.

I INSTANTLY knew the hundreds of uses for this thing, and went and bought one.

It can hold an upper kitchen cabinet in place, freeing BOTH of your hands. The cabinet is only leaning on the wall. So you can adjust it left and right, and for level. Then you still have 2 hands to drive in the screws. Easy!

This guy is using one to hold crown molding.

I remember a BAD job from my early days. I was installing a new medicine chest. It was such a heavy chest that I removed the mirror. It was still too heavy. I actually had to ask the lady to help hold it! Lucky for me she was a young babe, and not an old lady. It would have been impossible to hold the chest in place with one hand while I screwed in the screws with my other two hands.

My third hand can hold it against the wall with. I would not bother to remove the door.

It can hold it there, hands free. Now, is it centered over the sink? Is it high enough that you can see the top of your head in the mirror? Is it level?

Then you can use your two remaining hands to screw in the screws.

Even if the chest isn't very heavy, it's still a difficult job to do without the third hand. You can pre-start the screw, so you only need two hands. You hold the chest against the wall, check its height, check the level, pick up your drill, and the chest slips. Put down your drill and try again. And so on.

They have a short version, too:

But the only use I've ever found for this one is installing range hoods! It's either too tall or too short for everything else. And it costs almost as much as the long one, too.

# How To Replace A Faucet

I don't do most plumbing. I hate it. Maybe because I'm bad at it.

But I WILL install a new vanity. Hooking up the faucet is almost as easy as hooking up a garden hose.

### Old Faucet Removal

Sometimes, a basin wrench is not enough to remove the old faucet. I even walked away from TWO jobs in my early days, telling the ladies to get a real plumber.

Now I carry a piece of pipe, about a foot long, that I slip over the basin wrench's handle. Now even the hardest ones are easy.

### The Goal

I want two new supply lines, the silver braided kind. The top end of the supply screws on to the faucet. The bottom screws onto the emergency shutoff valve.

If I see the right supply lines already in place, I just attach the faucet and I'm done.

Sometimes you find hard copper supply tubes. Sometimes they are exactly the right length for the new faucet. I found this twice. In both jobs, the old risers leaked, and I had to return. For free. Now I ALWAYS use new flexible supplies. I like the ones with the silver braiding. If they are the older smooth ones, I replace them, too.

### Shut Off Valves

What? No valves? I install new shutoff valves. They really should have them, and now you have a nice place to attach the bottom end of the supply.

If an old shut off valve is just too hard to turn, you can buy a new valve and just put the new handle and valve stem. That old sweated on fitting is just fine.

## Compression Fittings

I always use compression fittings. They work fine. And there's no chance of burning someone's house down with a torch.

Use a small tube cutter to remove the old valve. There is always trouble getting the standard one to swing all the way around.

I carry two each of:
  "1/2 Compression inlet / 3/8 compression outlet" and
  "3/8 Compression inlet / 3/8 compression outlet"

These cover the two common sizes of copper pipes.

Here's a tip on compression fittings: Some people put a wrench on the fitting and tighten it as hard as they can, using both hands and all their strength.

These people often destroy other soldered fittings farther up the line. Sometimes the damage is INSIDE the wall!

The proper way is to use TWO wrenches, opposing each other. Also, when you grab both wrenches with both hands and squeeze, your grip is pretty strong and you have good leverage.

## Supply lines

I buy
  "1/2 FIP to Faucet  3/8 compression to valve outlet", 20 inches long.

I don't use the compression fitting on the top of the valve. Toss the nut and the compressing ring. Or throw them in your box-of-stuff. But the threads on the top of the valve are the perfect size for my supply line.

20 inches might be too long, but you get no prize for getting the perfect length. If it's too long, just make a loop.

# *Cheating At Plumbing*

You might be called to replace a leaking P-trap.

Leaking? They won't call until the P-trap is eaten all the way through, and you will find a bucket under the P-trap.

If you were called to replace the faucet, you should replace the P-trap, too. If it's all white plastic, it's still good. If it's shiny chrome on the outside, it's rusted on the inside, for sure.

You can replace it all with plastic. You can buy a kit that has everything you might need.

**FERNCO!**
OR, you can buy a FERNCO!

Fernco is a brand name. There are others.

It's flexible. Your pipes don't have to line up perfectly.

You slip it over the pipe, then tighten those two screw clamps. Done.

If you remove the upper clamp, you will see it gets a little smaller at the top. There are two sizes of down tubes in sinks. If you have the smaller down tube, you're good to go. The smaller section fits the smaller pipe. If you have the larger down tube, cut off the small section, and all that's left is the big section. Again, you're good to go. The larger section fits the larger pipe.

Do you want more good news? If there is a hair clog, you don't need drain cleaner. You just need a good squeeze or two!

Even MORE good news??? If the lady drops her diamond ring down the drain, she can remove this thing by herself! She doesn't have a pipe wrench, and wouldn't know which way to turn it. She won't even try. But THIS! THIS is EASY! She has a screwdriver. She doesn't even have to undo both clamps! Just the bottom on, then bend it and tip it into a bucket.

**SharkBite!**

Here's another plumbing trick:

Step one: You push that brown plastic end over your pipe.

Step two: You are DONE!

That orange thing is a removal tool, if you need it.

They have elbows, T's, unions and every other fitting.

They cost about $5 bucks each, so you'd never do a whole house like this. But for one or two, you can't beat it.

# PART FIVE

# MARKETING

## *Ten Lessons*

### Stop reading!

YES!!! You should wait until you have done a few gigs before reading the FIRST lesson.

Get all the basics out of the way first. Put an ad on craigslist. Load your tools into your car. Get the lady to sign on the dotted line. Go assemble some furniture. Get a few bucks in your pocket.

Ancient Chinese Proverb that I just made up:
He who reads all of these lessons before getting started is only procrastinating.

### Don't Even START Reading!!!

Remember what I said in the beginning about delegating? You should do what you're good at, and delegate the rest.

You should ask your wife to be your marketing manager!

She can bring more bucks into the household budget by keeping you busy than she could EVER make as a cashier or greeter somewhere.

This is ESPECIALLY true if you hate reading. Because if that's the case, your marketing won't get done at all!

### Read One Lesson At A Time.

Please do not read all of these lessons in one sitting.

You should read one, and stop.

Let it sink in. Do the homework. Do what it says to do.

Read the next lesson in a few days, or in a week.

### The Ten Lessons

Lesson 1     Introduction

Lesson 2     The Income Formula

Lesson 3     Set Up Your Web Site

Lesson 4     Increasing Your Number Of Customers

Lesson 5     Set Up Your Email List

Lesson 6     Set Up Your Newsletters

Lesson 7      Increasing Your Income Per Job

Lesson 8      Specialize

Lesson 9      Avoid Being Flagged On Craigslist

Lesson 10     Summary

# *Lesson 1: Introduction*

**Marketing 101**

Does This Sound Familiar?

You are on a job, and you are happy. You enjoy the work. You like being busy. You are thinking about the job, and on what's the next step.

But then the job ends, and you realize you have no more jobs lined up. You were NOT thinking about marketing.

So you start marketing. Maybe you call a few old names to scare up some business. Maybe you renew your ad in the Pennysaver, even though it won't appear until next week.

This feast-and-famine mode is killing you. If only you could develop a constant stream of jobs.

**Or How About This?**

You place your ad in the Pennysaver, and you do get some calls. But it's not enough to keep you busy. And you wonder if the ad is worth its cost.

My Pennysaver charges $35 a week for a tiny ad, and you must commit to 13 weeks, too. What if one week you only get ONE job, and only earn $100. It doesn't sound like it's worth it, but you have to advertise SOMEWHERE or you won't get ANY work.

And how many of those customers never call you back? You always remember to say, "If anything breaks, call me." But they seldom do. Maybe by the time something breaks they forget all about you. And when other tasks come up, like assembling furniture, you don't come to mind, because they think of you as the guy who fixes broken things.

**Marketing FACTS!**

You could read 100 marketing books (and most of us would rather be working on a job than reading even ONE book), and they would all say the same thing. These facts have been proven so many times, you cannot question them.

*Delegate:* Do what you're good at, and delegate the rest. This old rule REALLY applies to marketing! If YOU would rather be working than reading, maybe your WIFE should be reading this part! She could be your marketing department! She can be on the phone, making appointments, doing the marketing and monitoring the advertising. She can bring more money into the family budget by keeping you busy all week long than if she took a job somewhere.

*Consistancy:* You can't work for a while, then market for a while. You must market ALL the time.

*Repeat Business:* It's easier and cheaper to get repeat work out of an old customer than it is to find a new customer.

*Upselling:* If a woman calls you to install two miniblinds, should you refuse the job because it's too small? Maybe you should go and look for other things that need to be done. Expand a one-hour job to three hours. And develop a relationship that yields repeat business.

*A List:* You need a prospect / customer list.

*Hit your list:* You need to send out an email REGULARLY! You must stay in their face. When something breaks, they will remember you. And they will see the other jobs you do. Someone who called you to fix something may not realize that you also hang drape rods, install new mailbox posts, hang ceiling fans, install bathroom grab bars, etc.

*Lifetime Value Of A Customer:* That $100 job you got from a $35 Pennysaver ad was barely worth the effort. But it might grow into a much bigger relationship. If that customer calls you back for another $100 job, and then for a $1000 job, was that $35 ad worthwhile? What if they call you back every 3 or 4 months FOREVER! NOW how much did that $35 ad earn?

*Tracking:* When you send out an email, how many people open it? So how can you know if it's worthwhile? How many people called you on your Pennysaver ad? How will you know which advertising is worthwhile?

*Targeted Advertising:* You could put an ad on TV. It's expensive, and a lot of people will see it. But how many people will be looking for a handyman when they happen to see your ad? And how many will remember your TV ad when they DO need a handyman? It's better to place a smaller ad in a smaller market that is a BULLS EYE! What if someone did a Google search for a furniture assembler, and they saw your Google ad for furniture assembly? They see your ad EXACTLY when they want what's in your ad. What if you had a hundred little ads: one for drywall repair, one for powerwashing, etc.

*Unique Selling Proposition:* If there are ten handyman ads in your Pennysaver, some people will call the first one, and some will call them all and use the cheapest. You have to stand out. You have to be different.

*Specialize:* You can be the expert in one field. You don't have to be the jack-of-all-trades. Don't you see garage door companies? Gutter guard companies? Railing companies? A one-man-show can beat them. Gutter Helmet offers a $500 coupon and a payment plan. I wonder what their job costs! What if you could do the job for $1000, pay $200 for materials, and make $800, in only 4 hours! You could quit the "call me if anything breaks" business. Some specialties are better than others, because it's easier to target the customers.

## It All Comes Together

You have a web page.

People who click on your Google adwords ad come to that page.

People who see your craigslist ad come to your web page, too.

Your business card and truck sign mention your URL (your web address)

You have a list of email addresses. You email to them regularly.

People become aware of all the jobs you can do.

# Lesson 2: The Income Formula

There is a formula that you can use to calculate your income.

You can also use the formula to PREDICT your income. If you are thinking about making some changes in how you advertise or how you work, you can see in advance how these changes would affect you.

You can also use the formula to PLAN your FUTURE income.

Quite a formula! But when you see it, you will poo-poo it, saying it's too easy, and too obvious.

Yet I bet you started your career without thinking about the formula. You just placed an ad to see what would happen. You had no idea if this new career would pay off. You just gave it a spin to see where it would go.

Here's the Formula:

**Annual Income =**
**Number of Jobs per Client x Number of Clients x Average Income per Job**

Drag out some paper and a pencil, so you can follow along using your own numbers.

## Think Annually

You might think in terms of monthly income or even weekly income. But for this, it's best to use a whole year.

Some weeks are better than others, so it's hard to calculate your income per week. To figure your average weekly income, you need your annual income anyway.

Some handymen are into big jobs, like remodeling. Some jobs take more than a week. And the Number of Jobs per Client is less important. Once a person gets their kitchen remodeled, they are unlikely to need another kitchen remodel again next week. You might eventually go back and remodel a bathroom, but your client is probably tapped out right now.

## The Power of Multiplication

These marketing lessons will teach you how to increase all three factors.

If you DOUBLE any factor, you will DOUBLE your entire income.

If you DOUBLE two factors, you will QUADRUPLE your income!

And if you DOUBLE all three, you will be making EIGHT times as much as you made before.

## Example

Let's say you think you are finding enough jobs by advertising in the Pennysaver. (Your local throwaway might be called the Thrifty Nickel, the Weekly Shopper, The Green Sheet, etc. Everyone gets it for free every week whether they want it or not. It has lots of ads and is stuffed with flyers for pizza, dry cleaning, etc.)

Let's say you attract 200 customers. That's 4 per week.

But people RARELY call you back. In order to keep this example simple, let's say NONE of them EVER call you back. You go on a job and you NEVER hear from that lady again. I know that's unreasonable. But let's keep this example simple.

So your Number of Jobs per Client is 1.

And let's say you make $100 per job, on average. Of course, you have expenses. You have to pay for your Pennysaver ad, you have to drive to each job, and so on. But let's save that for later.

So this example's base line annual income is 1 x 200 x $100 = $20,000. One job per client, 200 clients a year, $100 per job.

It's nothing to write home about, but it's more than you could make as a cashier somewhere. And you're only working 4 jobs a week. Not even half-time.

What if you learn how to get callbacks? Now, some clients will NOT call you back, no matter what you do, and others will call only once, and a few will call you regularly. But to keep the math simple, let's say that each and every client will call you back once. So you have 2 jobs per client.

Now your annual income is 2 x 200 x $100 = $40,000.

And what if you could also increase your number of customers? You can advertise somewhere else, or several other places. Let's say you double your number of customers.

Now your annual income is 2 x 400 x $100 = $80,000.

Finally, let's increase the income per job. You go to a house and do the job they requested, but then you walk around the house with the client and find other things that need done. OR, you realize you are charging too little and all you have to do is increase your rates. Whatever. Let's double the income per job. You might not be able to double your income per job, but in keeping the math simple, let's say that's exactly what you do.

Now your annual income is 2 x 400 x $200 = $160,000.

A More Reasonable Example

It's unlikely that ANY of those factors will double, let alone all three. There might not be enough hours in a year to let you do 800 jobs worth $200 each.

It's also unlikely that all three will go up the same amount.

Let's try it again with some realistic numbers. Let's say you are making $40,000 a year, and you get that by earning $200 per visit, and you have 200 customers who only call once and you never hear from them again. You have a handful of people who call you 2 or 3 times a year, but you don't have enough to raise your average much.

This is totally reasonable. If you advertise in your Pennysaver, you will attract people. 200 customers is only 4 per week.

If so, your formula is 1 x 200 x $200 = $40,000

If you get only ONE factor to go up by only 10%, your entire income will go up by 10%! Let's say you do some different advertising and you attract only twenty more customers. Remember, that's only 20 more customers IN A YEAR! Now you have 220 customers. Entirely reasonable.

Now your formula is 1 x 220 x $200 = $44,000! That's a $4,000 raise! That's a 10% raise!

Your buddy with a desk job WISHES he could get a 10% raise. And all he can do to get it is work hard and hope his boss notices. And he can hope and pray. YOU, however, can DO something to MAKE it happen!

ANY improvements you make in ANY factor will improve your total income!

## The Power Of Compounding

AND what if you increased your number of visits per customer? Regular email advertising can do that easily. By keeping in their face, people will remember you when they need something. And some people will see something in your newsletter and they realize, "Hey, I didn't know you did that!"

If you could only get 20% of those customers to call you twice, that "1" increases to a "1.2", and your formula becomes 1.2 X 220 x $200 = $52,800!

Wait a minute! Read that again!

All you have to do is find 20 more customers A YEAR? And get only 20% of your customers to call you twice A YEAR? And your income jumps from $40,000 to $52,800? And we didn't even touch your rates???

So we increased one factor by 10%, and another by 20%, so your income jumped by 30%, right? Not exactly! Thirty percent of $40,000 is $12,000, which would only produce $52,000. You see? $52,800 is actually a 32% raise! The 10% factor increased your total income by 10%. The 20% factor increased your total income by 20% AND increased that 10% increase by 20%, too!

So the important point is this:

### *ANY improvements you make in ANY factor will MAGNIFY any improvements in the other factors.*

## Planning Your Income

Calculate last year's income using that formula. You probably know what your annual income was, but it might take some record searching to calculate how many different clients you had, how many repeat jobs you had, and how much you made per job.

Now look at each factor.

Which factor is too low?

Which factor would be easiest to increase?

What would be a reasonable and achievable amount of increase?

Now recalculate what your new annual income would be.

Is this increase in income worth the trouble of increasing that factor?

Is it possible to increase TWO factors? All three???

While you are painting a bedroom or cleaning a gutter, the back of your mind should be spinning on this concept.

# *Lesson 3: Set Up Your Web Site*

## You NEED a web site!

Before you get into increasing each factor in the formula, JOB ONE is starting a web page! You cannot do any serious marketing without one.

Want proof? Name me ONE big company that doesn't have a web site! And big companies must know what they are doing. Otherwise how did they get to be big companies?

My Pennysaver only allows 15 words in my tiny ad. But if one of those words is my URL, I can speak volumes. With pictures!

Business cards and magnetic car signs don't give you much room either. Use the little room you have efficiently.

When you drive around, look for other handyman trucks. NONE of them have websites! You will be ahead of all of them!

## You Need A Landing Page For Google Adwords

Google ads are cheap. It only displays when someone searches for what you are selling. And it displays for free. You only pay when a person clicks. And the price for a click can be as low as 10 or 25 cents.

I have a Google ad for cutting up an old swing set for the trash. When someone searches for somebody to cut up an old swing set, they see my ad. Think about it. They see my ad EXACTLY when they are looking for me. (You can search for my ad, and you probably won't see it, since I restricted it to Pittsburgh.)

How much does it cost to keep this ad running? NOTHING! I pay only when someone clicks on the ad.

You can have LOTS of targeted Google ads. You can have one for drywall repair, one for cellar clean outs, one for ceiling fans, and so on.

But when that prospect clicks that Google ad, it has to link somewhere. You NEED a landing page. In fact, you need SEVERAL landing pages. The ceiling fan ad should link to a page about ceiling fans, not a page that also talks about cellar clean outs. You can do that with your FREE web page, by dedicating a Tab to each job.

## Good For Craigslist, Too

You can say more in craigslist ad than you can in a google ad, but it's best to say what people are looking for, then to direct them to your landing page.

## Your Website Must Build Your Newsletter Mailing List

You NEED a mailing list. When you send newsletters or emails regularly to your list, you "stay in their face."

Your customers will think of you when something comes up, and give you repeat business. It's all part of the formula.

You can start your list with your old customers and your friends and relatives.

Then what? How will it grow beyond that?

Your website should give visitors a place to add their names! Then your mailing list grows all by itself.

## You Need A Domain Name

Your domain name is your web address. It's what people put into their browser's address bar to go to your page.

My main website is at:
>       The-Honey-Do-Man.com

You can have any name you want, as long as nobody else has it.

If I could do it all over again, I would find a name without dashes. Dashes are hard to key into a flip phone.

My domain costs me about $15 a year. Peanuts, for the jobs it generates.

Some web hosters provide a free domain name, but they are awkward. I created a test account on WIX.COM, and they gave me:

>       Ken1115.wix.com/handyman

They only let you change the last part. I changed mine to:
>       Ken1115.wix.com/honey-do-man

They don't have to register that name. They already registered "wix.com", and the rest of that hooks on to their main name.

But look at it! If you're driving down the road and see it on my truck, would you remember it? Would you get it right when you got home and typed it in?

## You Also Need…

Drag and Drop – They all offer you an editor that lets you type your own text and import pictures.

Your OWN pictures – you will be sending out emails with your recent jobs, sometimes before and after pictures. A huge library might have a typical handyman installing a typical ceiling fan, but YOUR pictures are best.

Multiple pages – You must be able to create a page just about ceiling fans (or whatever you specialties are). A page just about ceiling fans works better than a huge page that include ceiling fans mixed into a ton of other stuff.

Direction to a landing page – People can go to your home page, and then click on the tab about ceiling fans. But your google ad about fans should ZING right to that page.

Bulk Mail – You need to send out your newsletters, to everyone on your list.

## Where Do You Go?

GoDaddy is big. You can get your own domain name, web hosting, and email for only $1 a month. But in the fine print, they jack up the price after the first year.

Google is REAL big. They have a website builder, too.

WIX.COM is big, too. You can get an absolutely free website, if you accept their free domain name. You can experiment with your free website as long as you like. You can edit your home page and add your extra pages. But before you buy your new truck sign, you should upgrade to the Non-Free domain name. Get your REAL name. You can send out 3 newsletters a month for free before you have to upgrade.

Free websites always put their own logo on your website. If "Powered by..." or a banner at the bottom bothers you, you will have to spend some bucks. I don't think your prospects will mind, and you shouldn't mind either.

## Let's Look At WIX.COM

You can do a search on "Free web site" or "web site builder" and find a TON. But I'm going to use WIX.COM as an example.

First, you have to create an account. Give a user name and a password. This is not your domain name.

Then you pick a category. I chose Business & services, Maintenance services.

Then you pick a template. It really doesn't matter. You can change EVERYTHING.

I chose Maintenance & services, handyman.

## Site Layout

I like a simple home page. It has to give your name, address and phone. And it can mention some things you do.

But the important thing is your specialty pages. One page about furniture assembly, and a DIFFERENT page about ceiling fans. Etc.

## Home Page / Header

That handyman in their template HAS to go!

• His tool belt is too new! It's not even dirty. I bet it still has the price tag.

• He only has two screwdrivers. No hammer. No pliers.

• He has three different rolls of tape, and no idea what each one is for. Pretty colors?

• And I bet he borrowed that six-foot tape measure from his wife's junk drawer.

Click on that picture. Delete it.

That logo has to go, too. This is several images. Several clicks and deletes.

Then you have to add a picture. Hit the PLUS sign to add something, and select "Image". You can choose from their pictures, or upload your own, or "borrow" one from images.google.com.

And you have to change text like your phone number. You can just click on their text, and replace.

You can add text to a blank spot, too, starting with that PLUS sign.

## Other Pages

Click each tab (services, testimonials, etc.) and edit that text, too.

## Add Pages

You need your own pages, too. Add one about ceiling fans.

Hit the "Pages" menu. It lists all your pages. At the bottom is a button labeled "+ Add Pages"

Add your page and name it. It appears as a new tab.

Now edit your page. Add pictures and text.

## Bulk Mail

We will add a form so visitors can add their email to your newsletter list, but we'll do while we're talking about the newsletter section.

## Do It Now!

Get this homework done NOW!

If you're just reading this book cover to cover, there's a huge danger that you won't actually DO any of this stuff!

And you need this website to do the next steps. If you just keep reading, you'll be back here pretty soon.

# Lesson 4: Increasing Your Number Of Customers

Do you remember the formula?

**Annual Income =**
**Number of Jobs per Client x Number of Clients x Average Income per Job**

We are going to start with the second factor, the number of clients. You get new customers from advertising. We are staring with the second fact because this topic is easy, and it provides more immediate results than the other two factors.

Word of mouth is the best advertising. It's free. It's also the most effective. What a customer's best friend says about you weighs a LOT more than what you can say about yourself. I have gotten calls from FRIENDS of people who get my newsletter.

But you can't wait passively for that to happen. You have to take control, and place your own ads.

The next best and cheapest is a magnetic car sign. And of all the handyman trucks you see around, YOURS is the only one with a URL. See how this all fits together?

Business cards are cheap, too. Always leave them at every job. And if someone asks you about a job, hand them a card, and point out your URL. There's not much room on a business card, but you can say as much as you want on a web page.

## Google And Bing

Imagine a person wanting their gutters cleaned out, and they do a google search, and they see your ad for gutter cleaning!

Is that targeted marketing or what! You are hitting EXACTLY the person who has clogged gutters, EXACTLY when they want to do something about it.

You see these ads all the time when you search for something. They are the ads that run down the right side of the page and sometimes the first 2 or 3 lines at the top of the listings.

How much does it cost? It's FREE to appear in the list. You only pay when someone clicks. And you could pay as little as $1 or even 50 cents per click. When they click!

Compare that to an ad in my Pennysaver. They charge me $35 a week, for a tiny 15-word ad, and I have to commit to 13 weeks. I have to hope that someone goes to the Handyman section, and reads all the ads in that section, looking for gutter cleaning. I can put more than gutter cleaning in my ad, but not much. If I put my name (The Honey-Do Man counts for three words), my URL, my phone, "insured", my Pennsylvania registration number (required here), and "Gutter cleaning", I used 9 words, and I only have six more words left. I do a LOT of jobs. There's no way I could list everything. A person MIGHT go to my URL, but remember, they are sitting in their LazyBoy watching TV. And most people don't even read the Pennysaver at all! They don't call it a "Throw-Away" for nothing!

When they do a Google search, they are already AT their computer! They don't even have to enter your URL. They just have to click. And a full page appears dedicated to gutter cleaning! Say as much as you want! Show before and after pictures of a dozen jobs. Offer a coupon. Say you will also snake their downspouts. Try THAT in a Pennysaver ad.

And when they see MY page, they also learn about gutter fillers! "Never clean your gutters again!" He was looking for a $50 gutter cleanout, and I'm upselling him on a $700 gutter filler job.

You can have one ad for gutter cleaning, another for furniture assembly, and so on. You can have a TON of ads running for lots of little things. I even have one for cutting up old swing sets. It only hits once a year. But when it hits, I have a job. And when it doesn't hit, it's FREE. Try THAT in a Pennysaver ad.

And my Pennysaver lets me run my ad in five zones. Each zone includes several zip codes. But if I want to blanket the city, it would cost and arm and a leg. Did you ever wonder why the full page ads are always pizza shops? Because they are fine with local advertising. They don't WANT to blanket the city. A Google ad DOES blanket the city. In fact, if you don't restrict it geographically, it blankets the entire country. We will limit our ads geographically. You don't want to pay for clicks to clean gutters 2,000 miles away.

Everything here also applies to Bing, a newer search site run by Microsoft and Yahoo. But these instructions are targeted to Google.

Don't Miss Your FREE Listings!

Do a Google search for "handyman" followed by your zip code. You will see "Places for **handyman** near...", and under it you will see several handyman businesses. You might even see a handyman only a few blocks from you! How did that guy get listed, and Google doesn't know about you???

Every business can have a FREE listing. You just have to sign up. Search for "google place page".

Then if someone searches for "handyman" plus your zip code, they will see you. Actually, you can specify your zip code plus 10 or 20 miles, so people searching in several zip codes will see you.

Paid ads have advantages. You can specify more key words, like "gutter helmet" and "furniture assembly". You can move higher up the list by bidding a higher price.

So which should you use? Why, BOTH, of course!

**Start An Account**

This lesson is rather computer-intense. If working a computer is not your best talent, ask for help. Ask your wife or your nephew, or hire a high school kid.

You might already have a Google account, for GMail or for something else. But you need to pay for these ads, so you will be adding some payment method.

## Start A Campaign

Go to adwords.google.com

Either sign in with your existing account, or create an account.

You need a campaign to contain all your Ad Groups.

I have several campaigns. One is for my local handyman business, where I try to find different handyman jobs. All these ads are limited geographically. I don't want to pay for clicks for people trying to find a handyman in a different city.

Another campaign is for this book. This one is NOT limited geographically. I want to attract handymen from across the country.

You should start with one group. All your ads will have the same settings.

Go to the "Campaigns" tab on the main menu bar.

Click on the "+ New Campaign" button. It's under the chart, which is all flat right now.

Campaign Name: Call it "Handyman". If you only have one campaign, it doesn't matter what you call it. But you might start another campaign for something entirely different someday.

Locations: This is where we restrict your ads geographically. Those bundles are too big. Click on "Select one or more other locations".

First, UN-CLICK the bundle that was automatically selected. Start with NOTHING selected.

There are two good ways to select your desired areas. One is to Browse. Click the plus sign next to United States, and it expands into a list of states. You can click an enire state if you want. For me, Pennsylvania is too big. So I clicked its plus sign, and the list expanded to all cities within the state. In fact, Pittsburgh is too big. They include the entire southwestern corner of the state, and some of the included places are more than two hours away. If you expand a metro area, you see individual towns.

The other way is by a Custom selection. In fact, there are two good custom selections. One is a distance from a central map point. You can enter a zip code or even an intersection, then specify a distance. Try ten miles around your own zip code. If you live in a rural area, you might need to go farther than ten miles.

The other custom selection lets you draw a shape! This one is good if you want to avoid certain areas, or if you want to stretch a basic circle to include certain areas. This one is just cool to play with! Select "Custom Shape", zoom in until you see the area you want. Then start clicking to draw your selected area. Keep clicking until you can close your shape. You can drag those boxes to change your shape to include or exclude areas.

For me, I like to build big swing sets. I like doing it, and it's a big ticket item. I need a wider area for my swing sets. I don't mind driving an hour to get to a three-day job, but I do mind driving that far for a mini blind. So I need two campaigns, one for each distance.

Languages: You might want to include Spanish. They offer dozens of languages.

Networks: I like the Search Network. When someone does a search, I want to appear in the results.

I DON'T like the Display Network. When someone is looking at a related webpage for something else, your ad might appear on that page. I think this is not as targeted as when someone is searching for you, but that's just my opinion.

Devices: Do you want to limit to desktop and laptop computers? Or do you want to include iPhones? Smart phones have windows that are so tiny that viewing a normal web page is impractical. A person would have to scroll left and right so much that they would just quit in frustration. And then Google would say you have a high bounce rate, and your quality score will plummet, and your bid price will soar. If you want to allow smart phones, you should have a short and narrow landing page just for smart phones, and a more normal landing page for computers. This means two campaigns, two adgroups, and two ads, each with their own keywords. This is a lot of work. But you must decide. You cannot have smart phone users landing on your computer page and flitting away. Either exclude them, and lose business, or do the work.

Bidding Option: I like to set my maximum cost per click (CPC). If you are brave, you can let them determine what it takes to get good results. They may be good at what they do, but to me, this seems like letting your mechanic charge whatever he wants.

Budget: This is not a precise number; it's more like a monthly average. If you set a budget of $5 a day, that could be $150 per month. On the other hand, it might take you 25 to 50 clicks per day to reach that number. Let's say you DO get 50 clicks in a day. Do you want to close the door? What if those 50 clicks get you 5 jobs that get you $1000? May God smite you with that curse! However, if your ad is NOT working, you might not be getting ANY jobs for your $150 a month. More on this below.

Ad Extensions: You see this on huge sites. Search for ebay (don't go directly to ebay.com; just do a search). The results will have an entry for ebay, but underneath you see links for electronics, jewelry, etc. You don't need this feature yet.

## Start An Ad Group

An ad group for each job you do. I have one ad group for building a swing set, another for assembling a store-bought kit, and another for cutting up an old swing set.

Each ad group can have several different ads that appear, different keywords that people can search for, different bid amounts, and a different landing page.

I pay $1 per click for building a swing set, because this is my big ticket item. I pay less per click for my ad to cut up a swing set, because there is not a lot of competition, and I don't have to pay so much to appear at the top.

To create an ad group, click on the "+ New Ad Group" button. If you don't see it, click on the "Campaigns" tab on the main menu bar, then click on your campaign name on the left side.

Name: Give this group a name, like "build".

Create an ad: You create your first ad here. You can add other ads later.

Text ad: Start with a text ad. You're not big enough for images etc. Yet.

Headline and Description: These are very limited. The headline can only be 25 characters long. Each description line can only be 35 characters long. Bing considers the description one long line. Also, both must obey strict rules. You cannot have all capitals. One capital word for emphasis seems OK, and capitalizing the first letter of each word seems OK. But exclamation marks seem taboo.

Display URL and Destination URL: The URL displayed on your ad might be different from the actual link. My ad shows "The-Honey-Do-Man.com". But when someone clicks, it actually goes to "www.the-honey-do-man.com/playsets". This is called the "Landing Page". It's important that it relates to the intent of the ad group. My landing page talks only about swing sets. If it also talked about removing wall paper and cleaning gutters, Google would decide that my page is not relevant to swing building, and would give me a low quality score. More on this below. For now, just let your display and destination URL's both point to your web site. We'll come back and fine tune later.

Keywords: This is a list of what people might search for. If this ad group is about gutter cleaning, you could start with "gutter cleaning", "clean gutters", "clean my gutters", and so on. Think of EVERYTHING someone might search for. Then look to the right for more suggestions. And then click the "keyword tool".

Think creatively! Let's say you install gutter fillers or gutter helmets, which prevent clogged gutters. You might expect people to search for "gutter fillers" if they already knew about gutter fillers. But what if a person searched for "gutter cleaning" and they saw an ad for "Never clean your gutters again!"? So if your ad group is about gutter fillers, why not add MORE keywords for "clean gutters", etc. It doesn't matter that your ad is not about gutter cleaning. What's important is that you want people who are searching for gutter cleaning to see your ad about gutter fillers.

In fact, let's say someone is listening to the radio, and they hear an ad for Gutter Helmets. So they do a search to learn more. And THAT'S when they see YOUR ad for a different gutter filler. They had no idea that a better product could be a LOT cheaper! Thank you, Gutter Helmet, for paying for that radio ad!

For my swing set building ad, I don't expect people to search for someone who will build a new swing set from scratch. My ad group lists keywords for things like "assemble swing set". Hopefully, someone is about to buy a big kit from Toys-R-Us, but they won't buy it unless they can find someone to assemble it for them, and maybe I can switch them away from buying a flimsy cedar set. I tell them why "Cedar Sucks", prove that kits don't last, and then sell them on one of my pressure treated lumber sets.

You also need lots of keyword variations. I have "assemble swing set" and "swing set assembly". I also have "swing set", "swingset", and "playset". I also have singular and plural. All in all, I have 16 keyword variations. If someone enters "assemble playset" or "swingset assembly", I'm ready. You can have hundreds of keywords.

The keyword suggester suggested even MORE variations, like "Playset systems". I didn't choose that one, since it might include toys like Lego sets.

Multiple Ads

I have two ads for the same thing. One says:

**Rock Solid Swing Sets**
I Have PROOF That Cedar Sucks.
Don't Buy A Kit. They do not last.

The other one says:

**Cedar Sucks**
Don't Buy A Kit. They do not last.
I Build Rock Solid Swing Sets

Which one is better? I have no idea. But Google is figuring it out for me, automatically. When it's time to display my ad, they choose one randomly, and then track what happens. It's good if a person clicks, and not good if the ad did not make anybody click. And if they do click, then exit immediately because it is not what they expected, that's REAL bad.

Eventually, one ad will emerge as the clear winner, and it will be used all the time. The other one will still exist, but will fall into disuse.

## Quality Score

If someone searches for "gutter cleaning" and they click on my ad, and see my page about gutter fillers, they might stay there for quite a while. This is something new to them. And Google is watching, and gives that ad and that keyword a good score. But if they click to my page and immediately click away, because they didn't see what they expected, Google will give a poor score.

This is important to Google. Google is doing its job if people find what they are searching for. If Google sends them to an irrelevant page, they may soon get disgusted with Google.

It's also important to you. How high you appear in the list is very important. If you fall to the second page no one will see your ad. Just think about how YOU behave when YOU search for something. How many pages deep to YOU go?

Where you appear depends on the quality score of your keyword and on your bid. If you have a very poor score, you will have to pay a high bid to get good placement. If you have a good score, you can appear in the same position with a cheaper bid.

To see your quality scores, go to the "Keyword" tab, then on the next menu bar, select "Columns", and then "Customize columns". Choose:

Qual score: The quality score, on a scale of 1 to 10.

Est first page bid: Their (inaccurate) estimate of how much to pay to appear on the first page.

Clicks: the number of clicks

Impr: the number of impressions (how many times you appeared, whether someone clicked or not)

Cost: Your bill.

Avg Pos: Average Position - did you appear first? 12th (and therefore on the 2nd page?)

All these totals are for a week or a month or for whatever range you selected.

My "Assemble Swing Sets" keyword is my best. Its score is 7/10. It had 14 impressions and 2 clicks, so one in seven people click it. Its average position is 4.1. I should pay $.55 to be on the first page, but I'm paying $1, so I'm halfway up the first page.

Another keyword, "Assemble Swing Set", should be the same, but it's not. It's score is only 5/10. It only got 1 click out of 12 impressions, even though it's average position was 2.3 and the first page bid is only 30 cents. Go figure.

Both go to the same landing page, so the difference can't be there. It must be based on what people search for, and if they find what they were searching for. Or maybe 12 or 13 people is not enough people to make a valid study. Maybe it would be wise to look at a whole month.

The moral of the story is this: Take a chance. You can't go wrong. If you get no impressions or no clicks it costs you nothing. Let it cook for a week or two and go look at your results.

### Your Landing Page

To give people what they want, and therefore, to earn a higher quality score, and in turn, to pay less per click, you need a targeted landing page.

You can't have one big web page about everything you do, and have it target exactly what that person wants. You really should have one landing page about gutter fillers, another about furniture assembly, and so on. At least do 5 or 6 pages for your best specialties, and then let one more page catch the rest.

If you are using WIX.COM, each specialty page is a tab. A visitor can come to your home page, hit the "fans" tab, and see your page that's all about ceiling fans.

But you need the page address of each specialty page, too. Your google ad should zing to the fans page. You can't just jump your visitors to your home page and hope that they click on your fans tab.

I can jump directly to my WIX.COM fans page with this: http://ken1115.wix.com/honey-do-man#!fans/vb24m

Here's how to find that on WIX.COM:

1. Click the Pages drop-down menu from the top bar of the Editor.
2. Hover over the relevant page.
3. Click the Show More icon.

4.  Click Settings.

5.  Click the SEO (Google) tab.

6.  Click Preview on Google at the bottom of this tab.

Preview on Google

**mystunningwebsite | CONTACT**
http://supportkbtest.wix.com/mystunningwebsite#!contact
/c15n8
What makes your site unique? Describe your business and the
content on this page to visitors...

●

## Tracking

You can advertise in your Pennysaver, too. You might get big enough to place a 30-second spot on local TV!

But whatever you do, you must track. Which ads work and which don't? If an ad isn't working, you should quit paying for it.

Bing and Google already track for you. They tell you how many impressions (how many times it was shown) each ad got, and how many clicks you got. In fact, you could look into "conversion tracking". They can tell you when someone visits your page and actually does what you want them to do, like buy your product or send you an email.

Big companies spend a lot of time on this. Notice some ads on TV, for example. When you see the same ad on different channels, during different shows, or at different times, notice that the phone number and the URL are never the same. If you call a particular phone number, they'll know exactly where you saw the ad.

Maybe you are not that big (yet). But at least you can ask the person "Where did you see my ad?"

AND WRITE THEIR ANSWER DOWN!!! After a month or two you can analyze where your calls are coming from.

## Summary

The bad news is that this is a lot of work. In fact, you can't do this and forget it. You might have an ad in good position that's pulling well, but newer ads that are better push you down.

You can start with only one ad. Why not set up an ad for your favorite specialty? Set up other ads when you have some free time.

You should look at your results regularly. You might even avoid a billing surprise.

The good news is that this is cheap advertising. Even if you pay a lot, it's still cheap because you are getting a huge bang for your buck.

Now go back and repeat these steps on BING! They are almost identical! Google should sue bing!

## Craigslist

Craigslist is free, and easier to set up, but it's not as effective as Google adwords. If a person goes to Craigslist and searches for gutter cleaning, they may find you. But if they don't start with Craigslist, they will never see your Craigslist ad.

But it is free, so it is worth the trouble.

When you start advertising here, you'll see your ad on the first page for about ten minutes. So many people advertise here that your ad will be pushed down pretty quickly. Anybody reading all the ads will not read page after page of ads.

The good news is that people DON'T read the pages. They do searches. And a search will find your ad no matter what page it would appear on without a search.

Go to Craigslist now. Notice that they have one version for each city. That geographic limitation is already in place! Now notice that the default category is "For Sale". This is the perfect place to buy a bike. But it's not good for you to advertise gutter cleaning. That ad would get flagged because it's miscategorized. More importantly, people won't search in that category for gutter cleaning, so it doesn't matter if you manage to keep your ad listed or not.

The bad news is there are vigilantes out there who will flag your ad for other reasons.

Some of these reasons are only imagined. They are not in the Terms Of Use. I had an ad in the services / household section for TV wall mounts. I just placed another ad for furniture assembly in the same section. It was flagged. I have no idea why. Maybe it was a link to my landing page about furniture. No, that can't be it, because the first ad was not flagged and it has a similar link. They didn't give me a clue as to why it was flagged. Was it a Terms Of Use violation? And if so, which clause did I violate? Or maybe it wasn't that at all. Maybe it was flagged because it was miscategorized. So I went to their forum where you can ask "experts" why.

One said "It was because I had no price. Prices are required." Actually, that's not true. When you list something for sale, they want a price. There's even a box for it when you post. But not so with services. Go look. NONE of them have prices.

One said "You are only allowed one ad in one section in one city at a time." That's not true, either. I KNOW I had an ad for TV wall mounts AND an ad where I was selling my old ice skates. I found these phrases in the TOU:

"The same or substantially similar content may not be posted in more than one craigslist category." You can't post the same ad in two categories. I'm only using one category. And my ads are not the "same or substantialy similar".

"A user may post content only to the single specific geographic area". I'm only posting to Pittsburgh.

"A user may post the same or substantially similar content no more than once every 48 hours." This one says I am allowed to post the same ad every three days. My ads are different ads for different services.

People can see what they want to see.

Go to the "SERVICES" listings, and look at both the "household" and "skilled trade" sections.

Here's my OFFICIAL opinion why I was flagged:

1. There is no requirement for listing a price. Go to the services section and look. But there are a lot of people who think there is.

2. You are allowed a link. Go to the services section and search for ".org" and ".com". Now, there is a prohibition to some sites that provide hit counts and picture storage, but some people think NO links are allowed.

3. Choose some other imagined violation. It doesn't matter if it's legit or not. All that matters is a lot of people think it is forbidden.

If a lot of people flag you, you get flagged. And Craigslist doesn't ask them why they flagged you.

Go ahead and place an ad on Craigslist. But don't let your entire business depend on it.

# Lesson 5: Increasing The Number Of Jobs Per Client
## Part One: Your Mailing List

Do you remember the formula?

**Annual Income =**
**Number of Jobs per Client x Number of Clients x Average Income per Job**

The first factor in the income formula is the Number of Jobs per Client.

We are not talking here about making a job bigger by finding another other thing to do while you're on a job. We are talking about getting more jobs. Getting your existing customers to call you again. And again.

It's been proven time and again that it's easier to get an old customer to buy again than it is to get a new customer to buy the first time. In fact, the Direct Marketing Association says it's SIXTEEN times easier!

If you have 200 customers a year (that's only 4 a week), and if you can get 50 of them to call you just once more, your annual income jumps by 25%!

How can you get an old customer to call you again? The easiest way is to create a mailing list, and to send to that mailing list regularly.

When you did your last job, I'm sure you said, "If anything breaks, call me." as you drove off. That doesn't work. Well, it works once in a while, just enough to make you think it's working. But it's not really working.

When something finally breaks, 4 months from now, you will have left their mind. In that time, they will have forgotten all about you. Or they remember you but they forgot your name and they lost your business card.

When something comes up that is NOT a repair, like furniture assembly, you won't even be in their mind in the first place. They think of you as the "if something breaks, call me" guy.

Regular mailing will keep you in their face. When something finally breaks, they WILL think of you. You will still be in their mind.

And as you tell them about all the other things you do, you will get some "I didn't know you did that!" calls.

## TWO Lessons

This topic is so big that we broke it into two lessons. This lesson is about your list. How to create it, and how to grow it.

The next lesson will be about mailing out newsletters to your list.

This is not a spectator sport. It's important that you play along and actually create your list right now. Just like you built your website already, right?

Build your website. Then build your mailing list. You need to do both before you mail out your first newsletter.

Don't just read this and file it away for future use.

### The WORST Way To Mail To Your List!

It's easy to mail to a list. Just put all your email addresses in the TO field, separated by commas, and let it rip!

But the easy way is the WORST way! Every recipient will see all the email addresses. And each will see that you divulged their address to everyone else. Don't expect a thank-you note when they start getting a lot of spam. And when you only have ten customers, and they will all see that you only have ten customers, and, well…

### Blind Carbon Copies

A little bit better (a WEE little bit) is the blind carbon copy. Put your own email address in the TO field, and all the recipients in the BCC field (your email program might do things differently), and send it.

Nobody will see anybody else's address. Or how many you have.

### The BEST Way

The best way is to use a mailing company. They will send your email to everybody on your list.

Your emails will be beautiful. You can choose from many different templates. You will have pictures and colorful fonts. You just drag and drop your text and pictures.

Your emails will get opened! You can personalize the subject line. "Sharon! Here's Your Newsletter!"

They can track your emails! They know when someone opens your email. You get a report on how many people open it and how many don't.

Your emails will get through. If AOL or GMail think you are spamming, you will be placed on their black list, and NONE of your emails will get through. Emailing companies know what they are doing, and are actually on the white lists.

And they will maintain your list. People will be able to add themselves, and remove themselves, too.

These companies know the law. If someone wants out, and you send them an email anyway, you are spamming.

### Which Company

WIX.COM offers it, and calls it their ShoutOut. But as of this writing, they do not offer customization. And they don't maintain your list. And they don't track who opens your email.

It looks like WIX.COM concentrated on the website. It looks like emails were an afterthought. Maybe they'll catch up, in time. But at least it's free, for up to three mailings a month.

Other companies are iContact and AWeber. You can do a search and find many more.

## Start With Your Current Customers

Add your customers, friends, and family to your list. Add yourself, too, so you can see what you are sending to everybody else.

Our work orders have a space at the top for an email address. You should always ask for it. Many people will refuse, since they get too much email anyway. But tell them that it's only one or two emails per month, and there's always a coupon in it. If they still won't give one, give up.

## Generate your Signup Form

Your emailing company will give you a form to add to your web page.

People will fill in their name and email address, and hit a button that adds their info to your customer list.

If you are using WIX.COM, you have to install their "HTML iFrame/Embed" app.

When you add it to your website, a box appears. You can insert a web address or code. Choose Code, and paste in the form that your mailing list company gave you.

This ALL has to be in place for you to send out your first email.

At this point, you should have your website up, a mailing list company, and a form on your website where people can subscribe.

## Lesson 6: Increasing The Number Of Jobs Per Client
## Part Two: Your Newsletter Content

The whole point is to keep in their face. Think of it as giving them a business card every two weeks. Tell them the things you do, and you'll get some "I didn't know you did that!" calls.

Once a month is not enough. Once a week might be too much, both for you getting around to it every week, and for your customers getting so many emails that they stop opening them.

Maybe twice a week is ideal. Why not on the 15th and on the last day of every month. Kind of like when you had paydays, when you had a job, right?

You should carry a camera to all your jobs, which should be easy now that everybody has a smart phone. Take pictures of everything you do. BEFORE and AFTER pictures are good. Get a picture of an old ceiling light fixture, and a picture of the new ceiling fan that replaced it.

Always take a picture of a job, no matter how small. Take a picture of a doorbell button! There will be people who cannot or will not change their own button. Take a picture of YOUR OWN doorbell button. Even if you weren't asked to change anybody's button! Who will ask? Who will care?

Take a picture even if you have enough pictures ready for your next diary. Your next week could be dry, at least photographically speaking.

BEFORE and AFTER pictures are especially good.

Then you can tell everybody the jobs you did this week.
  "Here's an old swingset I cut up for the trash."
  "Here's a new baseball-bat-proof vinyl mailbox I installed, and the old rusty one I removed."

You will get some people who are so used to their old swingset and rusty mailbox that they don't actually see the problem anymore.

Include the same features in everynewsletter:

- What you've done lately. Or other jobs you CAN do, even if you haven't done them lately.

- You should add a joke, so people will look forward to your newsletter.

- And maybe a tip. Why not teach them how to do a simple job. Yes, it sounds like you are giving away your trade secrets. But you will look like a hero, like someone who is looking out for their best interests. Plus, when they screw it up, they'll call you for sure.

- And maybe a special deal or a coupon. Give $10 off or waive the trip fee if they give you a referral.

- Add a link to your web page.

Keep a notebook near your desk. Keep a list of jokes and tips, so when it's newsletter time, you'll always have one ready.

## Consistency

You want all your emails to look the same. You want consistency. It takes a little bit of work to add your logo, your name, your phone number, etc. to each email. So you do this only once, for your first email.

Then you can start your second email by re-using the first one. Replace the article and the joke. All your newsletters will look the same.

Most emailing companies have hundreds of templates. They were designed by professionals. They have beautiful backgrounds. But they do have a lot of things you don't need. You don't need a table of contents for all the articles in your newsletter if you only have one article. Choose any template you want as a starting point.

Think up a title for your newsletter.

Personalize it. Insert your name, phone number, and maybe your logo.

## Send Out A Test

Mailing companies let you have several lists. You might send one letter out to customers and a different letter out to prospects.

YOU will set up a list with only YOUR name in it.

Send your email out to that list, and they will only send YOU your email, and you can see what it looks like. If you screw up, nobody's the wiser, and you can fix your mistake and try again.

## Send Out Your First Newsletter For Real!

Next, you can let it rip and send it to everybody, or you can make a small change and do another test.

## Tracking

Wait a few days and see how you did.

Some mailing companies give you a list of all recipients, and show you who opened your newsletter.

They also show your bounces. That's the ones that couldn't be delivered. Bad email addresses and full mail boxes are common causes.

And your Unsubscribers. That's the people who you insulted with your crude joke.

## Future Newsletters

Mark your calendar to know when it's time to send out a new newsletter.

Re-Use an old email. Just change the content and pictures.

# *Lesson 7: Increasing Your Income Per Job*

Do you remember the formula?

**Annual Income =**
**Number of Jobs per Client x Number of Clients x Average Income per Job**

We covered the first factor. To increase the number of jobs per client, you start an email list that grows all by itself, and you send newsletters regularly to that list. If you keep in their face, they'll call you when something breaks. And if they see all the different things you do, they won't think of you only as the "Call me if something breaks" guy.

We also covered the second factor. To increase the number of clients, you advertise. Google is very effective and targeted. Craigslist is good too, and it's free.

## Two Ways To Charge

Now we move on to the third factor, increasing your average income per job.

There are two ways to charge for your work. Each has its own advantages and disadvantages. You might even be using both, depending on the job.

And each method has different steps to increasing your income.

## Charging By The Hour

I like to charge by the hour.

If all I did was install porch railings, I would REALLY know how much a given porch railing would take, and I'd know how much to charge for the job. But I do such a wide variety of tasks, I might only do one porch railing a year.

If you were to join one of those handymen franchises, they'd give you a sheet showing what to charge for everything, from toilets to mail box posts.

Now, some customers don't like the hourly basis. They feel they're writing a blank check. If I don't know how long a given job will take, how are THEY supposed to know? And if a 2-hour job grows to 10, they're looking at $400 or $500!

So when they are worried, I add a cap. "I think this job will take 2 hours, but we can limit it to 4. So if it takes more than 4, that's the maximum I will charge. But if it only takes two hours, that's all you'll pay for. It might cost as much as $200, but it will probably only be $100. You only pay for what you use."

I also explain it like this: "When a handyman bids a fixed price for a job, he always shoots high, in case something goes wrong. And if nothing goes wrong, he's the big winner and you're the big loser. He will bid that job as though it will take 4 hours. And if it only takes 2 hours, you're still paying as if it took 4."

I experiment with what I charge all the time. Currently, I charge $39 an hour, with a minimum of two hours.

I add $10 per hour for weekends and evenings. This usually hits double-income families who have too much money. If it's a single mom, I waive it.

I also charge a $25 service call. Don't call it a trip charge, or the lady next door will get upset. So a one-hour job costs $25 + $39 = $103.

## Increasing Your Income If You Charge By The Hour

If you are charging by the hour, just raise your price per hour.

If you are charging $35, why not try $39? What do you have to lose? You might have a few people go elsewhere. But there will be some people who think that's a fair price for good work.

In fact, you should always experiment with your price. If you NEVER lose a job, you are charging too little.

If you charge $49 and get enough jobs, you will know you are WORTH $49.

You can carry some $10/hour coupons. If someone objects, give them a coupon. Then you are charging only $39, but you are not losing the job.

If someone says they know somebody who charges only $20, what should you do?

You should walk away, and tell them "Good Luck!" Because that guy is only worth $20. You might even get a call back to fix the bad job and make it right.

And the $20 person might not even exist. The customer might be bluffing.

Or if there IS one, he's probably so busy that your prospect might not be able to get him.

And if there is one, should you compete by charging only $15? Where does it stop? At $10? You might as well get a job somewhere.

What would your prospect think? You are charging $49, and your competitor is charging only $20. What does that say? Would you WANT the work that a $20 person does? Maybe the work done by the $49 person is worth it! In fact, maybe the $20 per hour person works so slowly that the bills could be the same!

And whatever you are charging, you can add a service call. HVAC, plumbers, and many others do this. Why not you? You can always waive it if there is an objection.

If you give your estimate, and the lady says she wants to think about it, tell her this: "Lady, my bid is fair, and I can start right now. If you let me start right now, I will waive the service call fee. But if you make me come back twice, I can't do that."

And you should be charging a premium for evenings and weekends.

You should mark up your materials. If you buy a screen door for $300, should you charge your customer $300? Why not $400? They did not shop for it themselves because they had no intention of installing the door.

Get better prices by shopping around. Buy your tile at a tile store, etc. If you can buy that same door elsewhere for $200, why can't you charge the same $400 you would have charged had you bought it for $300?

You can also increase your income per job by increasing your hours per job. Whenever you go to a job, always ask if there is anything else that needs to be done. The woman will always say that there is nothing else. That's when you issue The Honey-Do Challenge. You offer to walk through the house with her, finding things on your checklist. You will find problems that she's gotten so used to that she no longer sees them. You will find improvements that she never thought of. You can find this checklist at

http://the-honey-do-man.com/book/challenge.doc

You will find everything from attic access to bathroom door hooks.

Here's the challenge: If you cannot find 10 things, you will do one thing for free. Don't worry. First, you will ALWAYS find ten things. Even if nothing is broken, you will find ten improvements or Pizzazz things, like brass house numbers. And second, YOU get to pick which thing gets fixed for free. It could be as small as tightening a drawer pull. Sometimes I stop counting at 9, just so I can do a small thing for free. One lady had a kitchen drawer front come off. It took me 2 minutes to attach it.

## Charging By The Job

The other common way to charge is to charge by the job. You look at a job, and make a bid. You win some and you lose some.

I have a friend who always charges by the job.

He can make $500 for a four-hour job. That's $125 per hour!

But sometimes that four-hour job grows to eight hours. Now he's down to about $60, which is still more than me.

But often he misses the job altogether. The customer gets two or three estimates, and might find someone for $400 or even $300.

He has to drive to the job to make his estimate. The person is always getting two or three estimates, so this first trip is pure overhead. Even if he gets the job, he usually has to come back another day to do the work. He can only start working right away, IF he is the last bid the customer is getting, and IF he is the lowest, and IF the customer doesn't say, "You are the lowest so far, but I'm going to think about it some more.", and IF he has all the tools he needs for this job in his truck.

Let's say the average drive is 30 minutes, or one hour for a round trip.

Plus you have to look at the job, take measurements, and talk to the homeowner. Let's add another half hour for selling.

And let's say he misses three jobs and finally gets the fourth one, on average. You CANNOT ignore those lost trips.

So that four-hour job actually cost him:

2 hours of estimating, measuring and bidding four jobs,

4 hours of travel to make bids on four jobs,

1 hour to travel on the actual work day,

4 hours of actual work

That's ELEVEN hours! Plus gas! How much gas does your truck burn in five hours? Five hours times 50 MPH is 250 miles. At 15 MPG, that's about 17 gallons. At $3.50 per gallon (as I write this), that's $60!

I NEVER go to a job just to look. I tell people my rate, guess how long the job will probably take, and when I get there, I start working.

But I could NEVER charge $100 an hour. People will think that's too much per hour, and compare in their minds what I am worth to what they are worth.

But my friend can charge it, because they are unaware of the price per hour. His customers think in terms of what the job is worth to them.

For instance, say it takes two hours to hang a basketball hoop. I could not get $200 because people will not pay me $100 per hour for that job. But they would pay my friend $200 because it's worth $200 to them to get that hoop up. They don't care what he's making per hour. What's important is what the job is worth to them.

### Increasing Your Income If You Charge By The Job

You can actually increase your income per job by DECREASING your bid!

This makes sense when you remember the jobs you lose because your bids are too high.

To understand this, just take it to the extreme. If you bid $1000 for a $200 job, you will NEVER get a job, and you will be driving around all day. NOW what's your income per job?

But if my friend would lower his bids, he could actually make more per job. If he gets one job out of two, then he's not wasting so many trips chasing jobs that he will never get.

Yes, he's making less per job, but he's getting more jobs, which is another factor in the formula. So he's actually increasing his income per year, which is the name of the game.

### Beginner's Advice

Why not charge by the hour for most small jobs, but charge by the job for one specialty?

For instance, search for "dryer vent cleaning". You will see companies charging $99, or $79, but nobody charges by the hour. If it takes you one hour, you could never get $99 for the job by the hour, but you could get it by bidding the job.

So go buy a dryer vent cleaning kit. It's a rotating brush and several flexible extension rods that attach to your drill.

Another good one is gutter fillers. And porch railings.

Learn what it costs for materials, do a few so you know how long it takes. Then make your bids based on what it's worth to the customer, and on what your competition is charging.

# Lesson 8: Specialize

Remember the Income Formula?

**Annual Income =**
**Number of Jobs per Client x Number of Clients x Average Income per Job**

I showed you how you can increase any factor, and you will increase your entire annual income by that percent.

And I showed you how if you increase two factors, they magnify each other. If you increase two factors by 20% your income jumps by 40%.

And I showed you how to increase each factor.

Here's another twist: Why not do bigger jobs? I like to build big swing sets. Each one takes three or even four days, but I make more on one job than I could earn in a MONTH at a McJob!

If all I did was build big swing sets, I would have:

- Only ONE job per client. People who buy my swingset NEVER need a second one.

- Very few clients. I can only hope for one client per week.

- But a very large income per job. They can cost up to $3,000. Each.

You see? You can increase each factor and your income will rise. But here we are actually REDUCING two factors, but that reduction is more than offset by a huge increase in the third factor.

## Specialties

Read your next Pennysaver, or notice the different trucks you see on the road, and different specialties will jump out at you.

I see trucks from several companies that install garage doors. What does that tell you? It says there must be enough business to keep several businesses busy. And they must be making enough money to pay a crew and pay for those trucks.

There MUST be enough money for little-ole you. You can ALWAYS beat a big company.

You can earn an embarrassing amount of money, if you figure it by the hour. So don't charge by the hour. Charge by the job. Remember, it's not how much you are worth per hour; it's how valuable this job is to the homeowner. For example, I can buy enough guttter filler to do a small ranch house for about $200, and it takes two hours to install. But I can charge $800 for the job. I can blow away Gutter Helmet, which offers a $500 coupon and a payment plan! And the homeowner hates ladders and wouldn't know where to buy the filler, certainly not at my price. And I'm making $300 an hour! You'll never get that much handymanning. You'll never get that by charging by the hour.

Look for jobs that don't require a special license. Forget plumbing and electrical.

And forget jobs that require a lot of training and a lot of tools. I include carpet installation in this category.

Look for something that the average handyman can do, but usually doesn't do. Maybe you have to do a few jobs to learn the ropes, or buy a special tool that you would never need again if you only did one job. Learn where you can buy your materials cheaper. Separate yourself from other handymen.

But above all, find something that the average homeowner cannot do for themselves.

## Swing Sets

As I've said several times, I like building big swing sets. Here's a link to my landing page:

http://the-honey-do-man.com/swingsets.aspx

I buy a kit that contains the brackets that connect the 4x4 posts together, the swings, the tarp roof, and so on. Then I buy the lumber locally.

The first one took four days. But now I've gotten it down to a science. I make some of it at home, then I bring these prefab pieces in my utility trailer.

I buy the kits from amazon.com. The big set costs me about $400, and sells for $1899, and takes me about 2 1/2 days.

I offer some options which can crank the price upwards of $3000. The options have a bigger bang for the buck. The best is the monkey bars, which cost $19, plus 6 2x4's cost $3 each, or $37, and sells for $148. The first one was clumsy; I was sure it couldn't be done by anybody with only two arms. But like I said, I got it down to a science, and it takes less than an hour.

I need minimal inventory. I have one kit of each size, and one of each of the accessories in my shed. When I get an order, I replenish my inventory.

## Porch Railings

Porch railing installation is a good example.

You can buy vinyl railings anywhere. But I have two railing places near me that sell a lot more stuff than most stores, and they sell it cheaper, too. Most stores only have 8-foot sections. A 9-foot span would require an extra post. But I can buy a ten foot section at these places.

You need a hammer drill, and you need a sawzall, and you might already have these. You don't need a ton of tools.

You don't even need a big truck. Railings do not come in big 10 x 3 panels. You get a top rail, a bottom rail, and a lot of balusters. I can get them in my minivan and close the hatch.

First, notice your own railing. Or your dad's railing. There's no better place to learn.

Also, you can call a railing company for a quote, to see what they would charge. For my own house, I needed about $400 in materials. Yet one company bid $2700! Even if I charged by the hour at $50, there's no way this job would take 46 hours! I declined. And a week later, they called back with a lower bid. Surprise, surprise.

When you are doing other handyman jobs, notice the railings. When you find an old rusty cast iron one, suggest a new railing. When they ask how much, stall them off. You need to measure, plan, price materials, etc. Think through the job and guess how long it might take. Figure one hour per section and one hour per post. Your estimate will be way high, and you will still be way lower than the other bids. But even if it takes you longer on your first job, you won't be losing money. Perhaps you made a pretty low wage per hour. But your next job will be faster, and you'll have a better grasp on how long each step actually takes.

When you do your first job, you will realize some tricks. Your second job will go faster. On MY first job, I learned:

I could rest a horizontal section on two 2x4 scraps. That held it in place and left my hands free while I attached the end brackets.

Everyone knows you should not cut the excess from one end; you should cut half of the excess from each end. That leaves a more balanced look. But what I learned was that you can slide the metal stiffener insert to one end. You only have to cut through the metal once. You are cutting only vinyl twice.

It doesn't matter whether you are doing garage doors or gutter fillers. Your first job will always go slower. If you specialize in something, you will get better.

If you do not specialize, if you do one railing job, then do one gutter filler job, you will not gain this advantage. Every job you do will be your first job.

One extra bonus: You can sell old cast iron to a salvage yard. See? If you do one railing job, it's not worth the trip. But if you specialize, and save old railings from several jobs, one big trip is certainly worthwhile.

## A Landlord Specialty

Here's one specialty that you won't find by reading the Pennysaver or noticing trucks on the road.

When a tenant moves out of a house or an apartment, someone has to go into that unit and get it ready for the next tenant.

A landlord with two or three units will usually do this themselves. There will be a few that would pay you, but it's hard to find them and they won't provide much work. They will only have one or two vacancies a year.

And forget the companies with hundreds of units. They have their own crews.

Consider a landlord with ten or twenty units. Some of these are investors with day jobs, and can't even do ONE unit for themselves. Even if they like to save money and do their own work, from time to time they will have several vacancies at once.

You would go in and toss trash and clean windows. Cleaning companies can do that, but as a handyman, you can do much more. You can put bi-fold doors back on their tracks, re-install drape rods that have pulled out, fix kitchen cabinet doors that won't stay closed, and paint over old food fights. The landlord doesn't need to call a handyman AND a cleaning company. You are a one-stop-shop.

You can walk through the unit with the landlord, suggesting things that would make the unit attractive to the next tenant. Suggest improvements, like ceiling fans, in addition to repairs.

Once you've done a few units, the landlord might even trust your judgment and give you a free hand, within reason. You know what jobs need to be done to attract a new tenant, and what jobs would be nice to do, but wouldn't actually attract any new tenants.

The main benefit to this specialty is that it's easy to find landlord customers, and you only need a few. You can go to a meeting of a landlord association. Look one up on the Internet. In fact, you should JOIN the landlord association.

Remember the income formula? One landlord customer is good for repeat business. And each job could go on for DAYS!

## TWO Realtor Specialties!

Realtors are also easy to find. But you don't want a company that's so big that they have their own crews.

In fact, you don't even want a company. All you want is an agent. And then another.

LISTING THE HOUSE

An agent will list the house. Then he/she will call you in. You, the agent, and the owners will all walk through the house together. You will suggest easy jobs that should be done. Your deal will actually be with the homeowner. The agent will encourage the owner to take your advice, and hire you to do some or all of the jobs.

You will see problems that the owner no longer sees. But people who see the house for the first time will certainly see these problems.

The homeowner will deny they need you.

For example, let's say you notice that the living room is dark and gloomy. Those draperies are so old they are probably original equipment. You suggest removing them altogether, including the drape rods, and installing some vertical blinds. The homeowner will always say, "How am I supposed to know what the new owners will want. Let THEM do it after they buy the house."

But people will NOT buy the house. The gloominess of the living room will turn them off. Do you think the homeowner is reluctant to install vertical blinds because they do not know the favorite color of the future owner? Or are they just making an excuse because it's easier and cheaper to do nothing?

Yet this small expense may cost them thousands in a lower offer, and it might take extra months to sell the house, which is another way to lose even more thousands.

## SELLING THE HOUSE

They will finally find a buyer, who will certainly do a home inspection. A dozen little things will turn up. Who else would they call? They will call a roofer for a new roof. But they will call you to fix the dozen little things. Would they call an appliance guy to fix a freezer handle, and a plumber to stabilize a rocking toilet, and an electrician to correct an outlet's reversed hot and neutral?

They are all little things, but they add up.

# *Lesson 9: Avoid Being Flagged On Craigslist*

## Craigslist

I NEED craigslist! As I said before, I like to sell my big swingset. I get some hits off my Google adwords, and some from craigslist.

I tried to expand my craigslist efforts, and get jobs for my gutter fillers and my furniture assembly.

AND I GOT FLAGGED!!!

When you get flagged, you get a nasty email, and they pull your ad.

I really don't care that my gutter filler ad got flagged. But I NEED my swingset ad! I can't afford to have THAT ad flagged! I GOTTA learn why I got flagged, and not make the same mistake on the swingset ad.

## Flagging

WHO FLAGGED ME! I got an email from craigslist that my ad was flagged and removed by craigslist! Not a clue as to who flagged me or why they flagged. What rule did I violate??? It does me no good when my ad is pulled. And I can't just repost it because whoever flagged it will just flag me again!

## The Forum

There is no help desk at craigslist. No one to complain to. All they have is a forum where you can ask other people what may have been the problem. These are not craigslist employees. They are volunteer users.

So I asked my questions. You show them your ad, and these helpers suggest what you might have done wrong. But these people were less than helpful.

For example, one person searched my other ads, and asked, "What are you trying to do??? Why do you have two ads posted at the same time?" Actually, this is not a violtion. The closest thing in the Terms Of Use is that you can't place the same ad every day. There must be a 48 hour delay. But these two ads were different.

Other people pointed out other apparent violations, which were not actual violations. And I tried to tell them how their objection was not an actual violation.

And one guy finally said, "Fine! If you're so sure that you're doing everything right, just keep posting your ad, and they'll just keep flagging it!"

I saw many ads that clearly violate the Terms Of Use that fly with no trouble. I see people place the SAME ad every day without being flagged, and my ad violated no rules, yet was flagged.

## The Missing Piece

I found another website that got into this a little deeper, and I finally learned something for the first time. Apparently all these "helpers" knew it. Rereading their comments, it is clear that they knew it, and they were assuming that I knew it too. Why didn't anybody tell me? Why didn't I know what I didn't know?

There is no craigslist employee flagging ads. Craigslist does not enforce their own rules.

For example, there is a rule against using another website to host your pictures. Don't ask me why this would bother them. But it is a rule. Now, if craigslist really cared about this, they could easily scan your code automatically when you post. It would be easy for them to look for "<a href=..." in your post, and AUTOMATICALLY tell you to remove that link before they post.

### Criagslist is "community monitored".

Here's how it actually works: You place your ad, and if someone doesn't like it, they can flag you.

I thought that flagging alerts craigslist, who investigates, and may decide to pull you. That's not it at all. Flagging only increments your flag count. When you exceed the flag limit, you get removed automatically, and get that email of death.

It also turns out that different categories have different limits! Even the same category might have different limits in different cities. And they won't tell what the limit is.

So it doesn't matter if you actually break a rule. All that matters is that someone THINKS you broke a rule.

It's not The Swingset Guy. It takes several flaggers to flag me.

I must be pissing off several people. Or is it MANY people? People click my ad, don't see what they expect, and BANG!

I guess you could just repost. It will take a few days for this new ad's flag count to reach its limit. But it would be better to solve the root problem.

### Reasons For Flagging

Go look at any craigslist ad. There is a link near the top, "Prohibited". Hover and see "miscategorized" and "spam", too.

Miscategorized - If you see an ad in a "For Sale" section for a person offering a service to assemble swing sets, you can flag him. He should place that ad in a "Services" section. I think I evade this one because I am SELLING a swing set.

Prohibited - no selling drugs, body parts, children, etc. I think I'm safe on this one.

Spam - Some people post their ad every day, to keep it on top. You see this often. You see an ad, and a few lines down you see the same ad. They are obviously reposting to keep their ad near the top. But why don't they kill the old ad?

This is my main frustration. I don't even know which of the 3 flags it was, let alone which rule I broke.

And I wonder if "The Swingset Guy" flagged me. He does not build my swingset. He assembles kits that people buy at Toys-R-Us. So he is not direct competition, but it's pretty close. Maybe I should flag HIM!

## Miscategorized

"For Sale" Is For Selling Things

That other website also identified my root problem! The "For Sale" category is for selling your old bird cage and your used ice skates.

YOU CANNOT RUN A BUSINESS IN THE "FOR SALE" CATEGORY!!! Not a handyman service. Not a gutter cleaning service. Not ANY service. You cannot even run a business selling things!

If your ad is full of colorful HTML fonts and imbedded pictures, BANG! They WILL flag you. People looking for an old bird cage don't want to wade through thousands of business ads.

## How To Survive

FIRST: Be in the right category.

Let's look at my gutter fillers.

I am selling something. So I have to go in the "for sale" sections. But would anybody be looking to buy gutter fillers? Most people don't know about them. Maybe a home handyman who knows about Gutter Helmet might be looking for some off-brand that does the same thing. But it's not likely. And if I taught him about gutter fillers, he'd go buy his own; not hire me.

I want to attract people who are looking for gutter cleaning. It has to be in the services section. And it has to look like "Gutter Cleaning". First, the homeowner will be looking for that. If he doesn't see it, he'll skip my ad. Also, the flagger must see gutter cleaning too. If he sees me selling something, I'm dead again.

So my ad does say "I'll clean your gutters." But it says "I'll clean your gutters ONE LAST TIME!" That sets me apart from the others, and makes the homeowner look closer.

SECOND: Make your ad look like the other ads. Use craigslist's pictures and fonts.

THIRD: You can't link to your website anymore. So I just say:
"Drag this URL to your browser's address bar:
www.The-Honey-Do-Man.com/swingsets.aspx"

You can't click on it. But people who want to see more swingsets will go to the trouble of dragging a URL.

## How To Thrive

When you post something (even your old bird cage), wait ten minutes and go look at the For Sale section. You are now tenth on the list. How will anybody ever find you.

They WILL find you, because nobody opens the For Sale section just to see what's for sale. They always search for something. And if they search for "bird cage", you will still be on top of the list tomorrow! Maybe even next week!

EMBED MANY SEARCH TERMS: I have "swingset", "swing set", and "playset". I don't have "play set" because that includes things like Legos. One is in the title, but the others are in the body, in normal looking sentences. Craigslist scans the title and the body. So if someone searches for any of these words, I will appear.

REPOSTING: Many people try to sell their old swing sets, so I do sink to the bottom pretty quickly. So every weekend, I delete my ads, and repost them. People don't see the old ad and the new ad at the same time, so they don't flag me for spamming. You can "RENEW" your ad. But that doesn't move you to the top. I think that just extends your expiration date.

I "DELETE" my ad. Then it lets me "REPOST". They remember my text AND my pictures. Now my NEW ad is at the top.

# *Lesson 10: Summary*

I hope you've been following along and doing the steps week by week. I hope you haven't been just reading along, because you would have a TON of work to do to catch up. And I hope you actually do these things, and not just put it aside for "some day".

Here's a summary of what we covered:

## Lesson 1 - Introduction

Marketing 101: Basic facts:

*Delegate:* If you're not good at marketing, or if you know you'll never get around to it, get your WIFE to do it! Get SOMEBODY to do it! SOMEBODY HAS TO DO IT!!!

*Consistancy:* You can't work for a while, then market for a while. You must market ALL the time.

*Repeat Business:* Get your old customers to call you again. Then get them to call you regularly.

*Upselling:* Take the small jobs, because you can expand them to larger jobs.

*A List:* You need a customer / prospect list. And you must get it to grow.

*Hit your list:* A newsletter gets your prospects to become customers, and your customers to repeat.

*Lifetime Value Of A Customer:* Don't worry if it costs you $35 to get a $100 job, because you can expand that job and get future jobs with that customer.

*Tracking:* Don't keep spending money on ads that don't work. Therefore you must track, to know what's working.

*Targeted Advertising:* Google adwords is the best. A customer searches for a furniture assembler and finds your ad for furniture assembly. Bulls Eye!

*Unique Selling Proposition:* What makes you different? If ten handymen all advertise for gutter cleaning, you are in a "who can charge the least" contest. So YOUR gutter cleaning ad sells gutter fillers.

*Specialize:* Get good at something. Learn the tricks, find the suppliers, buy a tool that most handymen don't have.

## Lesson 2 - The Income Formula

The income formula is:

Annual Income =
Number of Jobs per Client x Number of Clients x Average Income per Job

Part time example:

- One job per client. You never see these people again.

- 50 clients per year. One a week. Saturday mornings and you are DONE!

- 4 hours per job, times $39 an hour, plus $25 trip fee, that's $181.

That's $9,000 a year! You watched enough Saturday morning cartoons when you were a kid! $9000 is a down payment on a house. Most of a clean used car.

FULL TIME EXAMPLE: Crank it up to FIVE gigs a week. 250 clients per year. Now you're up to $45,000! Wait a minute. Did I say full time? And you're only working mornings? And you get Saturday's off???

Not bad. But you can do better.

We learned that if you increase one factor by 20%, you increase your entire income by 20%.

- You get 20% of your clients to call you once more. You see 50 people twice a year, and everybody else only once.

- OR, Your 250 clients increases to 300. That's 50 extra. That's one extra per week. Now you're working 5 mornings and one afternoon.

- Or, you increase your rate 20%. $39 goes to $47. If people think that's too high, bid jobs, and concentrate on a specialty.

Any one of these improvements changes your $45,000 to $54,000!

But if you could improve TWO or THREE factors, they magnify each other.

But HOW do you increase these factors?

## Lesson 3 - Set Up Your Web Site

You NEED a website if you want to get serious about marketing.

How do you get more customers? By advertising. But advertising is expensive. I can only put 15 words in my ad in my Pennysaver, but if one of those words is my URL, it can say as much as I want. Google advertising is CHEAP because it's so targeted, but you need a landing page for each ad.

How do you get customers to call you again? You need a list, and you must hit that list regularly. You need a website with a "subscribe to my newsletter" form. You need to tell your customers the many things you do, so you can get some "I didn't know you did that!" calls.

## Lesson 4 - Increasing Your Number Of Customers

How do you increase your number of customers? By advertising.

Google adwords is VERY effective. They are absolutely targeted. Imagine a person searching for gutter cleaning, and they see your ad. And your ad might be for gutter cleaning, or it might be for gutter fillers! "Never clean your gutters again!" They might even be searching for gutter helmet, and they see your ad as a cheaper and better alternative.

And this ad only cost $1! Or maybe only 50 cents! You only pay when a person clicks. You can have dozens of small ads. They lurk for free, until someone does a search. And a click.

It is a bit of work to set one up. But it's a lot quicker to set up your second ad.

And you DO need a landing page. So all those "URL-less" handymen you see around cannot play this game.

### Lesson 5 - Increasing Your Number Of Jobs Per Customer
### your list

You increase your number of jobs per customer by creating a list, and sending a newsletter to that list regularly. Keep in their face. They will remember you when something goes wrong, and they will see the many things you do.

Increasing this factor was such a big topic that it was split into two lessons. This lesson builds your list. The next lesson sends a regular newsletter to that list.

You should join an emailing company.

- They will maintain your list, and provide a form that you can add to your website where people can join your list.

- Your emails look beautiful, with a template, with pictures.

- Your emails get through. If AOL or GMAIL think you are spamming, they will "Black List" you, and NO emails will go through to those customers. iContact is on the white list.

- Your emails will get opened. The subject line says, "Hey Sally, Here's your newsletter".

- You get a report on how many emails get opened.

### Lesson 6 - Increasing Your Number Of Jobs Per Customer
### your newsletter content

In this lesson, we customized a template with your logo, name, phone number, etc.

Then we sent out your first newlsetter.

### Lesson 7 - Increasing Your Income Per Job

We explored the two main ways of charging: By the hour and bidding by the job. There are pros and cons to each.

And we looked into increasing your income per job, for each of those two ways of charging.

If you are charging by the hour, you can simply increase your rate. If you are charging $35 now, why not jump it up to $49? You might miss a few jobs, but you won't miss them all, and you'll make more per hour while you're out there. If you charge $49, and someone else charges only $20, who would the customer call? Who SEEMS like a better handyman? Who SOUNDS like they might screw up the job?

You can also increase your income per job by doing more things per job. You can go to a house to hang a drape rod, and while you're there you can get a bi-fold door back on the track.

You can increase your income per job by LOWERING your bids! If you're losing too many jobs because your bids are too high, you are wasting a lot of time and money driving to jobs that you will not get. You cannot ignore all that driving around. If you factor it in to the job that you DO get, the amount you actually earn per job is considerably less than what you THINK you are making on the job that you do get.

## Lesson 8 - Specialize

Another way to increase your income per job is to do bigger jobs. Specialize in something. Find a big ticket item that you can do, that you can get good at.

You will find better places to buy your materials. You'll know how long a job will take so you can make more accurate bids.

## Lesson 9 - CraigsList

How to survive on CraigsList and not get flagged.

## Lesson 10 - This Summary

This is not a spectator sport. I hope you've not just been reading along.

You CAN get customers to call you back for repeat business.

You CAN get more customers to call you in the first place.

You CAN earn more money per job.

Together, you WILL earn a LOT more money than you are making now.

At the very least, I hope I showed you that you could be doing more than running a Pennysaver ad and driving around with a magnetic sign on your truck.

There's a LOT to know about marketing. We have only scratched the surface. Even so, you will be doing more marketing that 95% of all handymen!

So quit reading! Go out and MAKE SOME MONEY!!!

# PART Ninety-Nine

## *Get started!*

I've done all I can. The rest is up to you.

Just do one job. Start with furniture assembly. You have everything you need. Bring a card table.

Place an ad in craigslist. It will hit. Maybe not today, but BE READY when it does.

When the phone rings, GO!

Assemble it. Put the money in your pocket. And THEN decide if you like this.

This can be VERY part time. What if you only want to do furniture assembly, and nothing else! What if you only get a call every two weeks?

If the average job takes four hours (sometimes you are asked to assemble more than one thing), and you charge $39 an hour, that comes to $4000 a year!

Or TV mounting. I charge a flat $99. Plus $25 trip fee.

But if you only did ONE job every two weeks, that's $3200 a year. And sometimes it's a person moving in, and they want two or even three TV's hung. Sometimes we add wire hiding.

Hey, $4000 here, $3000 there, it all adds up.

But it all starts with you actually getting out of your chair and giving it a try.


## *GOOD LUCK!*


Ken Whitaker, HDM

www.ingramcontent.com/pod-product-compliance
Lightning Source LLC
Chambersburg PA
CBHW08081318o526
45168CB00006B/2437